OUR 50 UNITED STATES
and Other U.S. Lands

THE UNITED STATES OF AMERICA

By the Editors of TIME FOR KIDS
WITH RENÉE SKELTON AND JAIME JOYCE

Collins
An Imprint of HarperCollinsPublishers

About the Authors: Renée Skelton often writes about America's past. She is the author of the TIME FOR KIDS® biography on Harriet Tubman and has a special interest in our nation's history and culture. Ms. Skelton lives in a historic town on the coast of our 3rd state (New Jersey).

Jaime Joyce was born in the 48th state (Arizona) and now lives with her family in the 11th state (New York). She has been interested in history for as long as she can remember and is ready to take a cross-country road trip to see the 50 states in person.

Collins is an imprint of HarperCollins Publishers.

Our 50 United States and Other U.S. Lands
Copyright © 2007 by Time Inc.
Used under exclusive license by HarperCollins Publishers Inc.
Manufactured in China.

Library of Congress Cataloging-in-Publication Data is available.

ISBN-10: 0-06-081557-4 — ISBN-13: 978-0-06-081557-8
ISBN-10: 0-06-081558-2 (lib. bdg.) — ISBN-13: 978-0-06-081558-5 (lib. bdg.)

1 2 3 4 5 6 7 8 9 10
First Edition

Copyright © by Time Inc.

TIME FOR KIDS and the Red Border Design are Trademarks of Time Inc. used under license.

Photography and Illustration Credits:
Credits run clockwise from top right of page except where noted. Cover photos: (flags) ImageClub; (Statue of Liberty) Digital Stock; (U.S.A. flag) Photodisc; (eagle) LLC, Fogstock/Index Open; p.1 top left: www.sos.state.mn.us; p.1 top right: Courtesy of the Missouri Secretary of State Office; p.2: Library of Congress; p.3: Library of Congress; Library of Congress; Library of Congress; p.4: Library of Congress; National Archives; Mansell/Time Life Pictures/Getty Images; p.5: Library of Congress; SuperStock; pp. 6–7 Joe Lertola; p.7: Library of Congress Geography and Map Division; p.8: AP Wide World; Library of Congress; Joel Sartore/National Geographic Image Collection; Delaware State Archives; p.9: Library of Congress; Library of Congress; Tim Laman/National Geographic Image Collection; AP Wide World; p.10: Johansen Krause/SuperStock; U.S. Department of the Interior, NPS, Edison National Historic Site; USFWS/Gene Nieminen; Library of Congress; p.11: Georgia Department of Economic Development; Francis Miller/Time Life Pictures/Getty Images; W. H. Duncan, University of Georgia Herbarium; Corbis; p.12: Tom Algire/SuperStock; Bettmann/Corbis; AP Wide World; Library of Congress; p.13: AP Wide World; Library of Congress; Library of Congress; Photodisc; p.14: Worldscapes/age fotostock/SuperStock; Alfred Eisenstaedt/Time Life Pictures/Getty Images; Damon Noe, The Nature Conservancy; Granger Collection, NY; p.15 top right: Raymond K. Gehman/National Geographic Image Collection; p.15 bottom right: AP Wide World; p.15 bottom left: John Jensen/Georgia DNR; p.16: Courtesy of the Naval Historical Center; NASA-JSC; A.H. Rider/Photo Researchers Inc.; Medford Taylor/National Geographic Image Collection; p.17: AP Wide World; Valentine Richmond History Center; Hugh Morton; Library of Congress; p.18: Library of Congress; AP Wide World; Robyn A. Niver/U.S. Fish & Wildlife Service; Richard Sisk/Panoramic Images/NGSImages.com; p.19: AP Wide World; Library of Congress; AP Wide World; Donald Uhrbrock/Time Life Pictures/Getty Images; p.20: AP Wide World; Library of Congress; Doug Perrine/SeaPics.com; Courtesy of Roger Williams University Archives; p.21: Michael Yamashita/National Geographic Image Collection; Richard Nowitz/National Geographic Image Collection; Mike Anich/age fotostock/SuperStock; Library of Congress; p.22: www.kentuckytourism.com; Picture History/Newscom; Tom Barnes, University of Kentucky; SuperStock; p.23: AP Wide World; AP Wide World; AP Wide World; p.24: AP Wide World; Steve Northup/Time Life Pictures/Getty Images; Joseph T. Collins/Photo Researchers Inc.; Print Collection, Miriam and Ira D. Wallach Division of Art, Prints and Photographs, The New York Public Library, Astor, Lenox and Tilden Foundations; p.25: Steve Vidler/SuperStock; Library of Congress; Shauna Ginger, USFWS; TIME FOR KIDS; p.26: AP Wide World; Library of Congress; L. West/Photo Researchers Inc.; Calumet Regional Archives, Indiana University Northwest; p.27: William Albert Allard/National Geographic Image Collection; courtesy of the University of Chicago Library; Suzanne L. Collins/Photo Researchers Inc.; Mary Evans Picture Library; p.28: Library of Congress; Library of Congress; AP Wide World; AP Wide World; p.29: AP Wide World; Library of Congress; James Henderson, Gulf South Research Corporation, http://www.gsrcorp.com; Alabama Bureau of Tourism & Travel/Dan Brothers; p.30: Jack Hoehn/Index Stock Imagery/Newscom; Alfred Eisenstaedt/Time Life Picture Collection/Getty Images; AP Wide World; Ingram Publishing; p.31: Library of Congress; AP Wide World; Harvey Mundy Hackett; Visions of America/Imagestate; p.32: Robert King/Corbis; AP Wide World; George M. Sutton/Cornell Lab of Ornithology; Arkansas Department of Parks & Tourism; p.33: AP Wide World; W. K. Kellogg Foundation; L. West/Photo Researchers Inc.; AP Wide World; p.34: NASA; John and Mable Ringling Museum of Art; U.S. Fish & Wildlife Service; Steve Vidler/SuperStock; p.35: Bob Daemmrich; Library of Congress; National Air and Space Museum/Smithsonian Institution; photo by Paul Cox, courtesy of the Lady Bird Johnson Wildflower Center; p.36: Iowa State Fair; AP Wide World; Douglas Graham/Wild Light Photography/Newscom; Francis Miller/Time Life Pictures/Getty Images; p.37: Library of Congress; Library of Congress; Kitty Kohout/Wisconsin Department of Natural Resources; AP Wide World; p.38: Robert Holmes/CalTour; AP Wide World; Steve Maslowski/U.S. Fish & Wildlife Service; courtesy of The Bancroft Library, University of California, Berkeley; p.39: Layne Kennedy/Corbis; by permission of Mayo Foundation for Medical Education and Research. All rights reserved; Thomas Barnes, Minnesota Historical Society; p.40: LLC, FogStock/Index Open; Library of Congress; Library of Congress; Dr. Louis M. Herman/NOAA; p.41: Bettmann/Corbis; Kansas State Historical Society; AP Wide World; PictureArts/Newscom; p.42: David E. Fattaleh/West Virginia Division of Tourism; Library of Congress; Joseph T. Collins/Photo Researchers Inc.; Library of Congress; p.43: Richard Olsenius/National Geographic Image Collection; courtesy of the Nevada State Library and Archives; James Morefield/Nevada Natural Heritage Program; Stewart Cohen/Index Open; p.44: AP Wide World; AP Wide World; Paul Fusco/Photo Researchers Inc.; Nebraska State Historical Society Photograph Collections, nbhips 10989; p.45: National Park Service; Library of Congress; Denver Public Library, Western History Collection; AP Wide World; p.46: Fred Hultstrand History in Pictures Collection, NDIRS-NDSU Archives, Fargo.; Denver Public Library, Western History Collection, D. F. Barry; Keith Frankki/U.S. Forest Service; AbleStock/Index Open; p.47: LLC, FogStock/Index Open; South Dakota State Historical Archives; AP Wide World; Denver Public Library, Western History Collection; p.48: Michael Melford/National Geographic Image Collection; Library of Congress; PictureArts/Newscom; Library of Congress; p.49: Greg Probst/Panoramic Images/NGSImages.com; 1996-98 AccuSoft Inc.; Raymond Gehman/National Geographic Image Collection; Mary Evans Picture Library; p.50: Silver Cloud Expeditions/Idaho Travel Council; AP Wide World; Jon Nickles/U.S.Fish & Wildlife Service; Courtesy Idaho Potato Commission; p.51: Raymond Gehman/National Geographic Image Collection; AP Wide World; Bill Pugliano/UPI Photo Service/Newscom; Denver Public Library, Western History Collection; p.52: AP Wide World; Picture History/Newscom; AP Wide World; Bud Freund/Index Open; p.53: AP Wide World; AP Wide World; S. Maslowski/U.S. Fish & Wildlife Service; AP Wide World; p.54: Steve Vidler/SuperStock; Allan Grant/Time Life Picture Collection/Getty Images; Tim Laman/National Geographic Image Collection; Jules Cowan/Index Open; p.55: Charlie Borland/Index Open; Arthur Schatz/Time Life Picture Collection/Getty Images; David M. Schlesser/Photo Researchers Inc; Photos.com Select/Index Open; p.56: National Park Service; Library of Congress; Jeff Schultz/Alaska Stock LLC; AP Wide World; p.57: AP Wide World; North Wind Picture Archives; Forest & Kim Starr; Library of Congress; p.58: Erwin Bud Nielsen/Index Stock; AP Wide World; p.59: AP Wide World; AP Wide World; p.60 top: Medioimages/Philip Coblentz/Punchstock; p.60 flag: ImageClub; p.60 bottom: Library of Congress; p.61: Granger Collection, NY; AP Wide World; p.62 top: Corbis/Punchstock; p.62-66: ImageClub; p.66 right: Library of Congress; p.70 bottom left: Iowa Department of Economic Development.

Acknowledgments:
For TIME FOR KIDS: Editorial Director: Keith Garton; Indexer: Marilyn Rowland; Art Director: Rachel Smith; Photography Editor: Jacqui Wong

 Read more about events in all the states of the U.S. at www.timeforkids.com

State Mottoes

"L'Étoile du nord (The north star)"
—MINNESOTA

"United we stand, divided we fall" —MISSOURI

"Labor omnia vincit (Labor conquers all things)" —OKLAHOMA

"Eureka (I have found it!)"
—CALIFORNIA

"Crescit eundo (It grows as it goes)"
—NEW MEXICO

"Hope"
—RHODE ISLAND

"Regnat populus (The people rule)"
—ARKANSAS

"Montani semper liber (Mountaineers are always free)"
—WEST VIRGINIA

CONTENTS

PART THREE

VOTES FOR WOMEN

The Story of the

This is a big country, with 50 states and nearly 300 million people. But it wasn't always that way. European settlement of North America began in the 1600s. A century later 13 British colonies had been established along the East Coast. But in 1775 American colonists rebelled. They felt that they were being treated unfairly by the British. It was the start of the American Revolution. A year later colonial delegates met in Philadelphia to write the Declaration of Independence. By 1781 the Americans had won the war, and the 13 colonies became 13 states, bound together by the Articles of Confederation. It soon became clear, however, that a strong federal government was needed. So in 1787 delegates met again to draft a new document, the Constitution. It laid out a plan for democracy. Continental Army commander George Washington became the first U.S. president in 1789. And the 13 independent states joined together by ratifying,

▼ America is named after Italian explorer Amerigo Vespucci.

▶ Free and low-cost land offers encouraged many settlers to move west.

or approving, the Constitution. By 1790 there were 13 stars on the American flag, one for every state in the Union. Since 1787, when Delaware became the first state, our country has grown by leaps and bounds. Thirty-seven states followed the original 13.

How to Become a State

The power for government to create new states is guaranteed by the Constitution. And while the first group of states was busy ratifying the Constitution, our country

▼ The United States Constitution

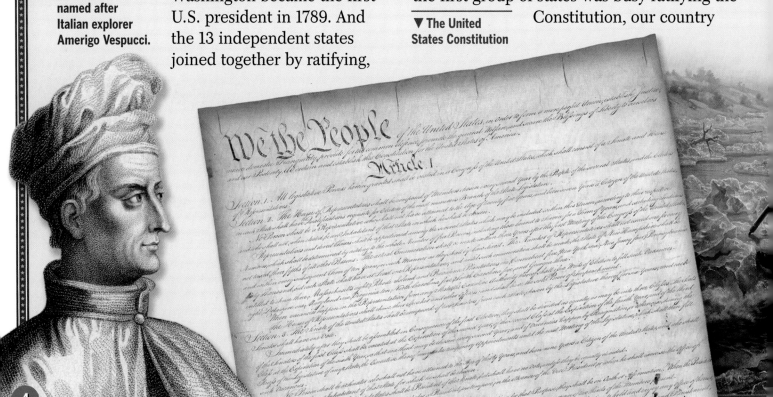

U.S.A.

► *American Progress* (1872) shows a woman, America, guiding pioneers and railroad trains toward the West.

gained more land. The Northwest Territory, around present-day Ohio, was so large that it was divided into several smaller territories.

The Northwest Ordinance laid out a plan for turning the territories into states. It gave the government the power to assign to the territories a governor, a secretary, and three judges. Once a territory had 5,000 white male citizens of voting age (women, African Americans, and Indians were not included in the count), the territory was allowed to elect its own legislature and send one non-voting delegate to the U.S. Congress. When the population reached 60,000, the territory could apply for statehood. But in order to do so, the territorial legislature had to write a state constitution, which then had to be approved by Congress. With the final authorization of the U.S. president, a territory could become a state. The Northwest Ordinance continues to guide the creation of new states. ✪

Manifest Destiny

The term manifest destiny was first used in the 1840s to describe our country's growth. Many Americans believed the U.S. would one day reach "from sea to shining sea." With the 1803 Louisiana Purchase, U.S. land stretched from the Atlantic Ocean to the Rocky Mountains. After the Mexican American War, in 1848, the U.S. expanded its reach to the south and west. Two years later California became the first state to border the Pacific Ocean. ✪

◄ In *Washington Crossing the Delaware* (1851) General George Washington leads Revolutionary War troops into battle.

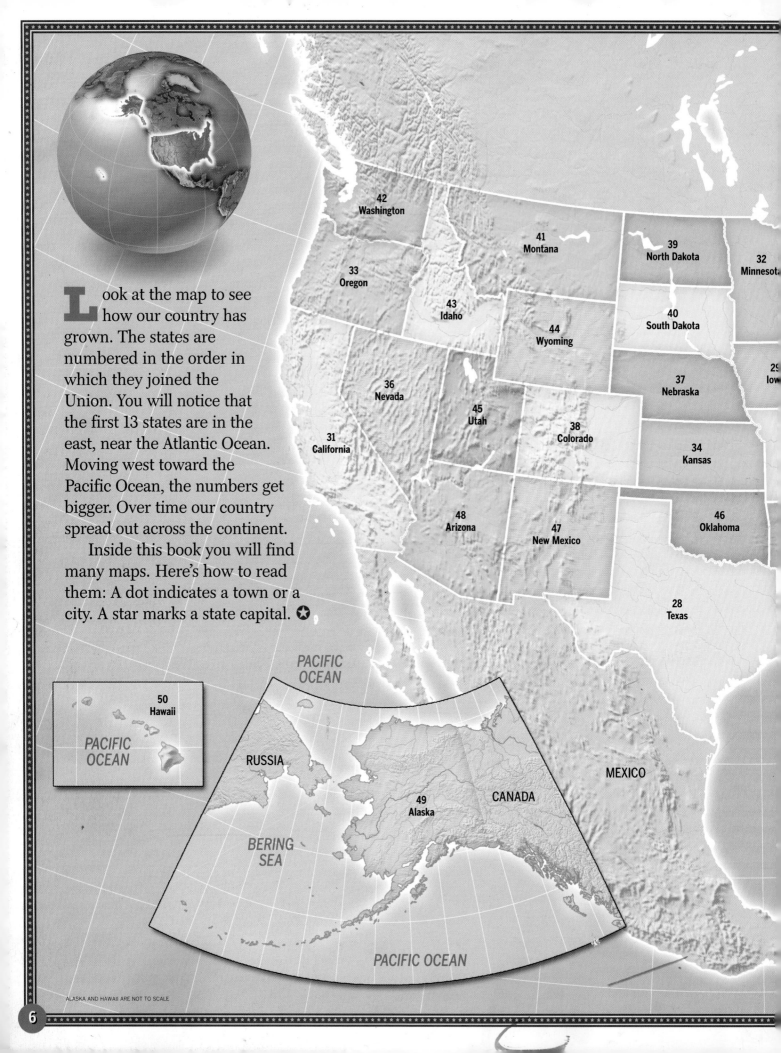

Look at the map to see how our country has grown. The states are numbered in the order in which they joined the Union. You will notice that the first 13 states are in the east, near the Atlantic Ocean. Moving west toward the Pacific Ocean, the numbers get bigger. Over time our country spread out across the continent.

Inside this book you will find many maps. Here's how to read them: A dot indicates a town or a city. A star marks a state capital. ✪

42 Washington

41 Montana

39 North Dakota

32 Minnesota

33 Oregon

43 Idaho

44 Wyoming

40 South Dakota

29 Iow

36 Nevada

45 Utah

38 Colorado

37 Nebraska

31 California

48 Arizona

47 New Mexico

34 Kansas

46 Oklahoma

28 Texas

PACIFIC OCEAN

50 Hawaii

PACIFIC OCEAN

RUSSIA

49 Alaska

CANADA

MEXICO

BERING SEA

PACIFIC OCEAN

ALASKA AND HAWAII ARE NOT TO SCALE

CANADA

LAKE SUPERIOR

LAKE HURON

LAKE MICHIGAN

LAKE ONTARIO

LAKE ERIE

30 Wisconsin

26 Michigan

21 Illinois

19 Indiana

17 Ohio

2 Pennsylvania

24 Missouri

15 Kentucky

35 West Virginia

10 Virginia

25 Arkansas

16 Tennessee

12 North Carolina

20 Mississippi

22 Alabama

4 Georgia

8 South Carolina

18 Louisiana

23 Maine

14 Vermont

9 New Hampshire

11 New York

6 Massachusetts

13 Rhode Island

5 Connecticut

3 New Jersey

1 Delaware

7 Maryland

ATLANTIC OCEAN

27 Florida

BAHAMAS

GULF OF MEXICO

CUBA

JAMAICA

N W E S

BACON'S
MILITARY MAP OF THE
UNITED STATES
SHOWING THE
FORTS & FORTIFICATIONS

On this 1862 map Union states are green, Confederate states are pink, and "border states and territories" are yellow. Border states were slaveholding states that did not secede.

Civil War

1861 *to* 1865

Less than a century after our country was founded, the issue of slavery threatened to break it apart. Slavery was important to the southern economy. Enslaved people worked the farms and the plantations. Many whites in that region believed they had a right to own slaves. Most Northerners disagreed. They spoke out against slavery. To them it was morally wrong.

Abraham Lincoln also believed slavery was wrong. When he became president in 1861, South Carolina protested by seceding from the Union. Soon other states seceded too. Mississippi, Florida, Alabama, Georgia, Louisiana, and Texas were first, followed by Virginia, Arkansas, Tennessee, and North Carolina. These 11 states banded together to form the Confederate States of America. Lincoln was furious. The Constitution made secession illegal, he said. But it was too late. The Civil War had begun. North and South fought against each other. In 1863, as the war raged on, Lincoln issued the Emancipation Proclamation, which put an end to slavery in the Confederate states. ★

Delaware

1st State ★ December 7, 1787

Delaware was a battleground in its early years—changing hands several times. Henry Hudson, a British explorer sailing for the Dutch, was the first European to see its coast in 1609. At the time, Nanticoke and Lenape Indians inhabited the area. In 1631 the Dutch built their first settlement in Lewes. However, local Indians burned it to the ground after a dispute with settlers. Swedish colonists established Fort Christina, now Wilmington, along the coast in 1638, but the Dutch soon chased them away. In 1664 the English captured the Dutch colonies of New Netherland (New York) and the Delaware settlements.

During the American Revolution, British troops occupied Wilmington for a few weeks. But no major battles took place there. In 1787

▶ The state is named for Thomas West, Lord de la Warr, Virginia's governor in the 1600s.

Delaware ratified the U.S. Constitution and became the first state of the new nation. Though a slave state, it remained in the Union during the Civil War.

Delaware is a state of north-south contrast. Starting in the 1800s, chemical manufacturing and research, shipbuilding, machine shops, and manufacturing plants grew up around Wilmington in the north. Today banking, insurance, and real estate companies are based there.

Southern Delaware is more dependent on agriculture. Poultry, soybean, and corn farms dot the rolling coastal plain. ✪

▲ The first log cabins in North America were built by the Swedes in Delaware about 1638.

Did You Know?

At its narrowest point, Delaware is just nine miles wide.

▼ A Delaware farmer tends her sheep.

Earth Alert! ▶
The Delmarva Peninsula fox squirrel lives in three states: Delaware, Maryland, and Virginia.

Mystery Person Born in 1730, this ▶ Delaware native was a member of the First Continental Congress. He rode his horse overnight from Dover to Philadelphia, PA, to become the first signer of the Declaration of Independence. He later served as Delaware's governor from 1778 to 1781.

ANSWER: CAESAR RODNEY (1730-1783)

Pennsylvania

2nd *State* ★ *December 12, 1787*

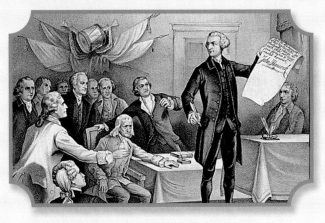

▲ John Hancock, president of the Second Continental Congress, boldly signed the Declaration of Independence on July 4, 1776.

The earliest people of Pennsylvania included the Lenape and Nanticoke Indians. The first European to see Pennsylvania may have been Henry Hudson, who sailed into Delaware Bay in 1609.

The Swedes established the area's first non-Indian settlement in the 1630s. The Dutch, in nearby New Amsterdam, took over the Swedish colony in 1655. The British then removed the Dutch in 1664.

Soon the British began to settle the colony. King Charles II owed money to William Penn's father, and he repaid it by granting Penn the land. Penn arrived in the colony in 1682. He was a Quaker, and he offered religious and political freedom to all settlers.

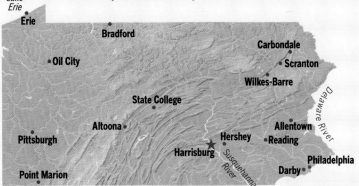

▲ Pennsylvania means "Penn's woods" after William Penn, the original proprietor of the colony.

Pennsylvania played a key role in the nation's early history. The Declaration of Independence was written in Philadelphia in 1776. The U.S. Constitution was written there in 1787. Pennsylvania became the second state when it approved the new Constitution that December. Between 1790 and 1800 Philadelphia served as the U.S. capital.

In the early 1800s, Pennsylvania's resources—coal, oil, iron—boosted industry. The state remains an industrial center today. But Pennsylvania is also an area of green pastures and corn fields. Its covered bridges, quaint villages, and 200-year-old homes are reminders of the state's historic past. ✪

◄ Philadelphia's Liberty Bell is an American symbol of freedom.

Did You Know?

Hershey, PA, has the world's largest chocolate and candy factory.

Earth Alert! ▶

The great egret was once hunted for its feathers. Now water pollution has damaged its natural habitat.

Mystery Person ▶ This

Pennsylvania reporter got a job at the Pittsburgh *Dispatch* after writing an angry letter to the editor. She gained fame in 1889 for a story she wrote for a New York paper about her trip around the world in 72 days, 6 hours, and 11 minutes.

ANSWER: NELLIE BLY (1864-1922)

New Jersey

3rd State ★ December 13, 1787

▲ The state was named after Great Britain's Isle of Jersey.

New Jersey's recorded history began in 1524 when the Italian sailor Giovanni da Verrazano explored its sandy shoreline. At the time, Lenape Indians lived in the area, hunting, fishing, and growing crops such as corn.

The Dutch placed their first settlement on the Hudson River in 1630, as part of New Netherland. In 1638 New Sweden was established on the Delaware River. The Dutch forced the Swedes out in 1655. But nine years later the Dutch lost New Netherland to the British.

King Charles II granted New Netherland to his brother James, Duke of York. James renamed it New York. He gave the land between the Hudson and Delaware Rivers to George Carteret and John Berkeley. They named their colony New Jersey.

During the American Revolution, American and British armies clashed more than 100 times in New Jersey, making it a major battleground. In 1787 New Jersey became the third state.

In the 1800s and early 1900s, millions of European immigrants came to New Jersey in search of factory work. Today industry remains important. With thousands of farms, colonial-era homes and mills, and more than 100 miles of beaches, New Jersey is a small state of great diversity.★

▼ The New Jersey Palisades rise above the Hudson River.

▲ General George Washington led American forces to victory in the Battle of Trenton on December 26, 1776.

Mystery Person On January 27, ▶ 1880, this inventor received a patent for the electric lamp, or lightbulb. His other inventions include the motion picture camera and the phonograph. Today, his labs in Menlo Park (now Edison) and West Orange, NJ, are national historic sites.

ANSWER: THOMAS EDISON (1847-1931)

Georgia

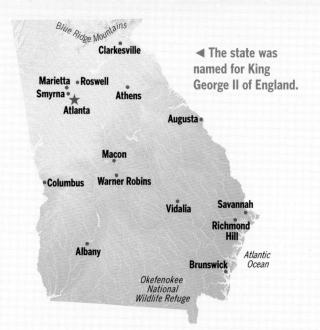

◀ The state was named for King George II of England.

When Spanish explorer Hernando de Soto arrived in Georgia in about 1510, he met Creek and Cherokee Indians in large villages farming corn, beans, and squash. Starting in the 1560s, the Spanish built settlements along the coast.

In 1732 King George II gave a group of Englishmen permission to start the Georgia colony. James Oglethorpe, the group's leader, wanted it to be a place where poor English people could start a new life. He led the first 120 settlers to present-day Savannah in 1733. Oglethorpe limited the size of farms and would not permit slavery. Eventually, both of these rules changed when the king took direct control of Georgia in 1752.

In 1788 Georgia became the fourth state. Cotton farming expanded—partly on land that Indians had occupied. The Creeks sold their land and moved west, but some Cherokee resisted. In 1838 U.S. troops forced them to move to Indian Territory (now Oklahoma).

Georgia fought for the Confederacy in the Civil War. In 1864 Union general William Sherman led battle troops through Georgia, destroying farms, factories, and rail lines.

Today Georgia's cotton farms exist alongside modern textile factories and chemical plants. Television production and broadcasting are centered in Atlanta, Georgia's largest city. ✪

▼ Historic homes are open to visitors in Savannah.

Did You Know?
Georgia grows more pecans and peanuts than any other state.

▲ President Jimmy Carter ran his family's peanut farm in Plains, GA, before serving as the state's governor from 1970 to 1975.

Earth Alert! ▶
The State Botanical Garden of Georgia is helping to restore endangered wildflowers such as the hairy rattleweed.

Mystery Person ▶
This civil rights leader was born in Atlanta. He helped to end segregation on city buses in nearby Montgomery, AL. In 1963 he gave his now-famous "I Have a Dream" speech in Washington, DC.

ANSWER: MARTIN LUTHER KING, JR. (1929–1968)

Connecticut

5th State ★ January 9, 1788

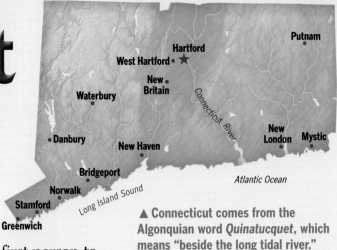

▲ Connecticut comes from the Algonquian word *Quinatucquet*, which means "beside the long tidal river."

Algonquian Indian groups called Connecticut home long before Europeans arrived. In 1633 the Dutch built a small fort where Hartford now stands.

But Connecticut's first permanent European settlers migrated from the Massachusetts Bay Colony in search of religious freedom. They established villages in the Connecticut River Valley and near Long Island Sound in the 1630s. These settlements became part of the Connecticut Colony in 1639. And by 1654 the English settlers had forced the Dutch out.

Most Connecticut colonists supported independence from Britain. During the Revolutionary War, the colony supplied beef, salt, flour, and gunpowder to George Washington's army. In 1788 Connecticut became the fifth state of the new nation.

Farming was important in Connecticut until the late 1800s. But local inventors helped industry grow as well. Eli Whitney, famous for his cotton gin, also made parts for guns. Eli Terry was the first person to mass-produce clocks. Bicycles, pins, and textiles were also made in the state. Connecticut's rivers powered its many factories, and after the Civil War European immigrants came to the state for work.

Today Connecticut produces hardware, aircraft parts, and submarines. Some of the country's largest insurance companies are based here too. Connecticut's small villages and old country lanes, which recall historic New England, make it a popular vacation place. ✪

▼ Inventor Eli Whitney attended Yale University in New Haven, CT.

Did You Know?

Connecticut created the first automobile law in the U.S. in 1901, setting the speed limit at 12 mph.

► The Mystic Seaport Museum preserves Connecticut's past. The area was once a major shipbuilding center.

Earth Alert! ►
The timber rattlesnake has lived in Connecticut since pre-colonial times. Today, the snake is endangered.

Mystery Person ►
This Connecticut mother of seven wrote a novel called *Uncle Tom's Cabin* (1852). It was about a slave mother, Eliza, who runs away when she learns that her child is about to be sold. The best-selling book was the most famous piece of anti-slavery literature in the 19th century.

ANSWER: HARRIET BEECHER STOWE (1811-1896)

Massachusetts

6th *State* ★ *February 6, 1788*

▶ The cranberry is a native American fruit. It grows in marshes, called bogs, throughout Massachusetts.

Though Algonquian Indians have lived in Massachusetts for more than 10,000 years, the state's written history began in the early 1600s when French and English ships explored and mapped the coast.

English Pilgrims seeking religious freedom established the first permanent settlement at Plymouth in 1620. The Massachusetts Bay Colony followed in 1630. But colonial leaders allowed only the practice of their own religions, so several groups left to start new colonies in present-day Connecticut, Rhode Island, New Hampshire, and Maine.

In 1691 the Plymouth and Massachusetts Bay colonies joined to form the Province of Massachusetts. It became a center for rebellion in the years before the American Revolution. Led by Samuel Adams and Paul Revere, colonists staged the 1773 Boston Tea Party to protest British taxes. Minutemen fired the first shots of the Revolution at Lexington and Concord in April 1775. After the war Massachusetts became the sixth state when it approved the U.S. Constitution in 1788.

Massachusetts's textile and shoe industries grew in the 1800s, with immigrants filling jobs in many factories. The state also became a center for whaling and fishing.

Today industry, education, research, and the arts thrive in Massachusetts. Its rich colonial history has made Massachusetts a favorite tourist destination. ✪

▲ The state is named for the Massachusett Indian people.

Map labels: North Adams, Amherst, Northampton, Great Barrington, Springfield, Worcester, Lexington, Cambridge, Lowell, Salem, Lynn, Boston, Quincy, Brockton, Plymouth, Fall River, New Bedford, Provincetown, Atlantic Ocean, Cape Cod Bay

Did You Know?
▶ Boston Common was set aside in 1634 by the town's government. It was America's first public park.

Earth Alert! ▶
Scientists have helped the American bald eagle make a comeback in Massachusetts. There are now 15 pairs nesting in the state.

Mystery Person
During the Revolutionary War, this Massachusetts teacher dressed as a man so that she could join the military. She called herself Robert Shurtliff and enlisted in 1782. A year later, she was honorably discharged when it was discovered that she was a woman.

ANSWER: DEBORAH SAMPSON (1760–1827)

13

Maryland

7th State ★ April 28, 1788

◄ Main Street in Annapolis has brick roads and colonial-style buildings.

Nanticoke and Piscataway Indians were living in Maryland when Europeans learned of the area. In 1632 King Charles I granted the lands of Maryland to Cecilius Calvert, Lord Baltimore. Colonists arrived from England two years later. They established the first permanent settlement at St. Mary's City. Calvert, who was Catholic, saw Maryland as a place where people could enjoy religious freedom, and in 1649 Maryland's leaders passed a law that granted freedom of religion to all Christians.

In 1788 Maryland became the seventh state when it approved the U.S. Constitution. It escaped most of the fighting during the American Revolution. But many battles occurred there during the War of 1812. On September 12, 1814, Francis Scott Key wrote the lyrics to "The Star-Spangled Banner" as he watched a British ship bombard

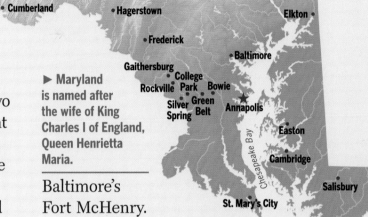

► Maryland is named after the wife of King Charles I of England, Queen Henrietta Maria.

Baltimore's Fort McHenry.

During the Civil War, Marylanders were divided. Maryland was a "border state," a slave state that remained in the Union. Still, many Marylanders fought for the Confederacy.

Maryland's industries expanded in the early 20th century, led by electronics, food products, and chemical manufacturing. Most industries and services are concentrated around Baltimore and near Washington, DC. But Chesapeake Bay—with its fishing, boating, and scenic shoreline—is an important area for businesses and visitors. ✪

▲ In 1763 Charles Mason and Jeremiah Dixon surveyed the boundary between Maryland and Pennsylvania. The Mason-Dixon Line marks the division between northern and southern states.

Did You Know?

Maryland is home to the nation's first school, King William's School (now Saint John's College), founded in 1696.

Earth Alert! ►

The sensitive joint-vetch grows near freshwater and partly salty marshes. Its leaves close at the slightest touch.

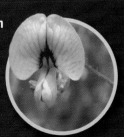

Mystery Person
A marine biologist and a writer, this Maryland resident wrote *Silent Spring* (1962). The book explained how pesticides can hurt plants and animals. It was a bestseller in the U.S. and Britain, and helped people to learn more about the environment.

ANSWER: RACHEL CARSON (1907-1964)

South Carolina

8th State ★ May 23, 1788

The Spanish were the first to explore the South Carolina coast in 1521. But they failed to establish permanent settlements. And though Sioux and Iroquois Indians already lived there, the English were eager for a foothold in the area. In 1663 King Charles II gave a parcel of land, which included today's South Carolina, to eight friends. They established the first permanent European settlement near Charleston in 1670.

South Carolina became a separate colony in 1729 and grew wealthy from rice and indigo plants, which were used to make ink. After the American Revolution, in 1788, South Carolina ratified the U.S. Constitution and joined the new nation as the eighth state.

The state's economy was based on large plantations worked by slaves. When Abraham Lincoln was elected president in 1860, some plantation owners feared slavery would end. South Carolina became the first state to leave the Union, in December 1860. Months later, on

▶ The state's name comes from the Latin form of the name Charles—Carolana—for King Charles II of England.

April 12, 1861, Confederate soldiers fired on Fort Sumter, touching off the Civil War.

Textile mills provided jobs in the late 1800s and early 1900s. After cotton crops were destroyed by insects called boll weevils in the 1920s, farmers began to grow tobacco and fruit. Today tourism, textiles, and wood industries are important to the state's economy. ★

▼ Myrtle Beach is a 312-acre state park.

▼ Peaches are one of the state's main crops.

Earth Alert! ▶
The flatwoods salamander comes out of its underground home to mate in the fall.

Mystery Person Raised in ▶
South Carolina, this painter decided when he was five years old that he wanted to be an artist. His paintings of American flags were popular in the 1950s. Today his work is on display in museums around the world.

ANSWER: JASPER JOHNS (1930)

New Hampshire

9th State ★ June 21, 1788

► The state is named for the English county of Hampshire, which was home to John Mason, the first proprietor of the colony.

Algonquian Indians lived in New Hampshire before European explorers, including Samuel de Champlain, arrived in the early 1600s. Several small settlements, such as Hilton's Point (Dover), Strawbery Banke (Portsmouth), and Exeter, were already established along its bays and rivers by the end of the 1630s. In 1641 New Hampshire became part of the Massachusetts Bay Colony. It was made a separate colony 38 years later.

New Hampshire was a strong supporter of the rebellion against England. In 1776, months before the U.S. Declaration of Independence was issued, the colony had already declared its independence. Even though no battles were fought in the state, hundreds of New Hampshire men fought in the American Revolution. After the war New Hampshire was the ninth state to join the Union.

During and after the Civil War, New Hampshire became increasingly industrial. Abundant water powered textile mills, and immigrants from Canada and Europe arrived to work in the state's factories.

During the two World Wars, the Portsmouth Naval Shipyard built submarines. Factories made uniforms and shoes for soldiers. Today a new electronics industry provides jobs. So does the tourism industry. New Hampshire's clear streams, rugged mountains, and colorful autumn leaves make it a popular destination for vacationers. ✪

Did You Know?

The highest wind speed recorded at ground level was at Mt. Washington in 1934 with speeds three times as fast as most hurricanes.

◄ Fall colors in the White Mountains

▼ A new submarine is launched at the Portsmouth Naval Shipyard, August 1935.

Earth Alert! ►
The Karner blue is New Hampshire's official butterfly. It feeds on wild lupine in the state's pine barrens.

Mystery Person In 1984 this New Hampshire high school teacher was chosen by NASA to take part in the next space shuttle mission. The *Challenger* took off on January 28, 1986. Sadly, it exploded 78 seconds after takeoff. All eight astronauts on board were killed.

ANSWER: CHRISTA MCAULIFFE (1948–1986)

16

Virginia

10th State ★ June 25, 1788

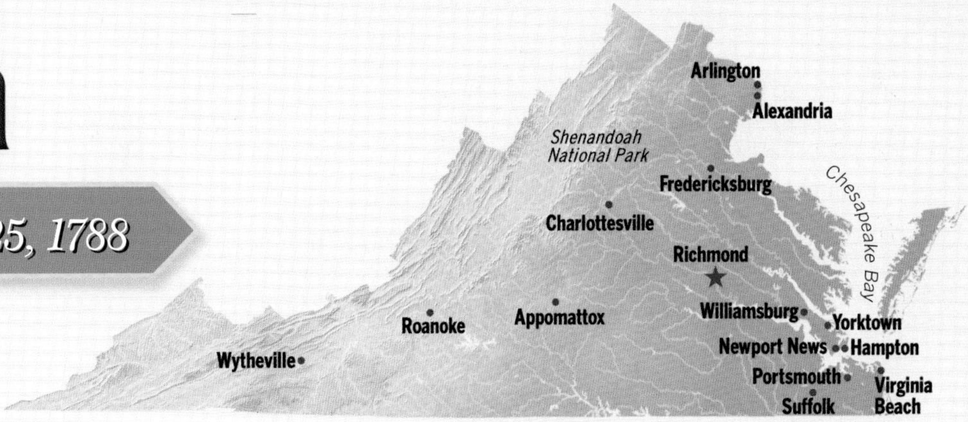

Map labels: Arlington, Alexandria, Shenandoah National Park, Fredericksburg, Charlottesville, Richmond ★, Roanoke, Appomattox, Williamsburg, Yorktown, Newport News, Hampton, Portsmouth, Virginia Beach, Suffolk, Wytheville, Chesapeake Bay

▲ The state was named for England's Queen Elizabeth I, who was known as the "Virgin queen" because she never married.

Powhatan and Cherokee Indians inhabited Virginia long before English colonization. In 1607 the first permanent English settlement in North America was established at Jamestown. In 1624 England made Virginia its first New World colony. Settlers struggled in the beginning. But they soon learned to grow food and raise tobacco, which they exported to Europe.

Virginians played important roles in early American history. Thomas Jefferson wrote the Declaration of Independence. George Washington commanded the Continental Army during the American Revolution. Many important battles were fought in Virginia. The British surrender, which ended the war, took place at Yorktown in 1781. Afterward, James Madison, a Virginian, helped to write the U.S. Constitution. In 1788 Virginia approved the Constitution and became the 10th state.

In the early 1800s, slave-dependent plantations expanded in eastern Virginia. When the Civil War began, Virginia seceded. But several western counties stayed loyal to the Union. These separated from Virginia to form West Virginia.

In the late 1800s and early 1900s, the state's tobacco, textile, and shipbuilding industries grew. Manufacturing, government, and farming provide jobs today. Tourism is important too. Visitors tour Virginia sites that preserve its rich history. ✪

Did You Know?

Virginia has had three capital cities: Jamestown, Williamsburg, and Richmond.

▼ The Richmond, VA, railroad station in 1865

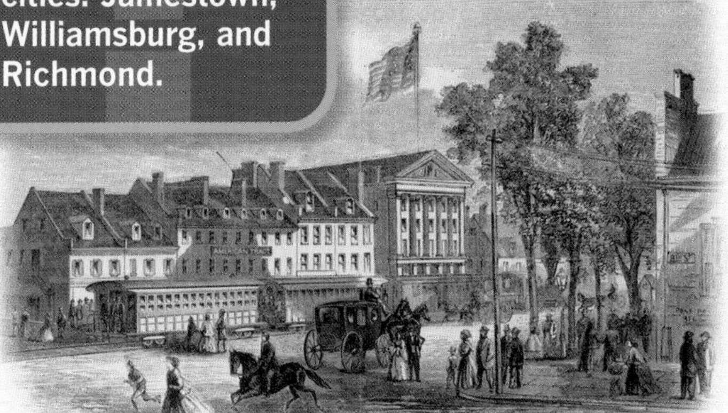

▼ The Chincoteague Island Pony Swim is a yearly event.

Earth Alert! ▶

Virginia big-eared bats live in limestone caves in the Appalachian Mountains. Their lifespan is 16 years.

Mystery Person
Some people called her "Crazy Bet," but this Virginia woman was very clever. She used her inheritance to free slaves. During the Civil War, she was a Union spy, gathering information to help defeat the Confederacy. Later, President Ulysses S. Grant made her Richmond's postmaster.

ANSWER: ELIZABETH VAN LEW (1818-1900)

New York

New York was the home of the Iroquois and several Algonquian tribes when the first Europeans arrived. Giovanni da Verrazano sailed into New York Bay in 1524. Henry Hudson explored the region for the Dutch in 1609. In 1624 the Dutch claimed the area as New Netherland and established their first settlement at Fort Orange (now Albany). The next year they bought Manhattan from the Indians and founded New Amsterdam, today's New York City.

In 1664 the British captured New Netherland and renamed it New York. They occupied New York City during most of the American Revolution. Still, important battles took place elsewhere in the state.

New York joined the Union in 1788. The opening of the Erie Canal in 1825 and the expansion of canal and railroad systems increased trade and helped industry grow. It also increased New York City's importance as a port and trade center. The arrival of millions of immigrants in New York City starting in the 1800s swelled the state's population. It also made the city a melting pot of many races and cultures.

Today New York is a center of trade, finance, communications, and industry. But the state still has huge areas of wilderness and many productive orchards and farms. ✪

Did You Know?
New York City was the U.S. capital between 1785 and 1790.

◄ An immigrant family at Ellis Island looks across New York Harbor at the Statue of Liberty.

▼ The state was named for the Duke of York, who received the colony from his brother, King Charles II.

Potsdam
Adirondack Mountains
Niagara Falls
Rochester
Buffalo
Syracuse
Utica
Schenectady
Lake Erie
Albany
Catskill Mountains
Jamestown
Poughkeepsie
Hudson River
Yonkers
New Rochelle
Mount Vernon
New York City
Montauk

▼ Niagara Falls, on the border between New York and Canada

Earth Alert! ►
The rare Leedy's roseroot grows in only two states—Minnesota and New York.

Mystery Person
This Brooklyn, NY, native was the country's first black Congresswoman. In 1968 she was elected to the U.S. House of Representatives, where she worked for 14 years to help the poor, minorities, and children. In 1972 she ran for president.

ANSWER: SHIRLEY CHISHOLM (1924–2005)

North Carolina

12th *State* ★ *November 21, 1789*

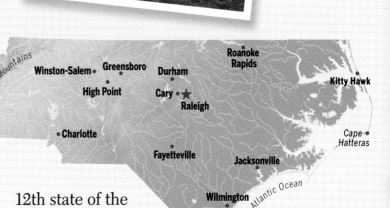

Cherokee and Tuscarora Indians were living in North Carolina when European explorers saw the coast in the early 1500s. The English established their first colony in North America on Roanoke Island in 1585, but they left the following year. The English tried again, leaving a new group of settlers on the island in 1587. A few of them returned to England for supplies. When they came back in 1591, they found the colony had vanished. The fate of this "Lost Colony" remains a mystery.

In 1663 King Charles II granted the land of the large Carolina territory to eight proprietors, or businessmen. North Carolina became a separate colony in 1712. And after the Revolutionary War, the British lost their claims. In 1789 North Carolina became the 12th state of the new nation.

Although it was a slave state, North Carolina was reluctant to leave the Union even after the Civil War had begun. But after it joined the Confederacy, the state gave the rebellion strong backing.

In the early 1900s, North Carolina developed textile, furniture, and tobacco industries. These industries are still important today. But North Carolinians also look to computers, banking, education, and tourism for a prosperous future. ✪

Winston-Salem • Greensboro • Durham
High Point • Cary ★ Raleigh
Asheville
• Charlotte
Fayetteville • Jacksonville
Wilmington
Blue Ridge Mountains
Roanoke Rapids
Kitty Hawk
Cape Hatteras
Atlantic Ocean

▲ The state's name comes from *Carolana*, a Latin word that is a reference to King Charles II.

▲ Men move rocking chairs at a North Carolina furniture factory.

Earth Alert! ▶

Packs of red wolves live in North Carolina's Alligator River National Wildlife Refuge.

Mystery Person

This bicycle mechanic and his brother, Orville (right), built America's first airplane. They tested it near Kitty Hawk, NC, on December 17, 1903. The brothers made four flights that day. His was the longest. It lasted 59 seconds.

ANSWER: WILBUR WRIGHT (1867–1912)

Rhode Island

Narragansett and Wampanoag Indians lived in Rhode Island thousands of years before Italian explorer Giovanni da Verrazano saw its shore in 1524. In the 1600s, it became a haven for independent people with unpopular ideas. The leaders of the Massachusetts Bay Colony expelled Roger Williams for disagreeing with their rules. He headed south to Narragansett Bay. There Williams founded Rhode Island's first permanent European settlement, near today's Providence, in 1636.

When the American Revolution began, hundreds of citizens volunteered to fight. After independence was won, Rhode Island was the last of the original 13 colonies to approve the U.S. Constitution. It joined the Union in 1790—but only after a promise that a Bill of Rights would be added to the Constitution!

The textile industry began in Rhode Island in the late 1700s when America's first water-powered cotton mill was built in Pawtucket. The nation's jewelry industry began in Rhode Island in the 1790s. The state remained a leader in these industries well into the 20th century.

Narragansett Bay has been an important shipbuilding and trade center in Rhode Island since the 1700s. Today it shows Rhode Island's unique ocean character, with naval facilities, shipping, fishing, and other water activities. ✪

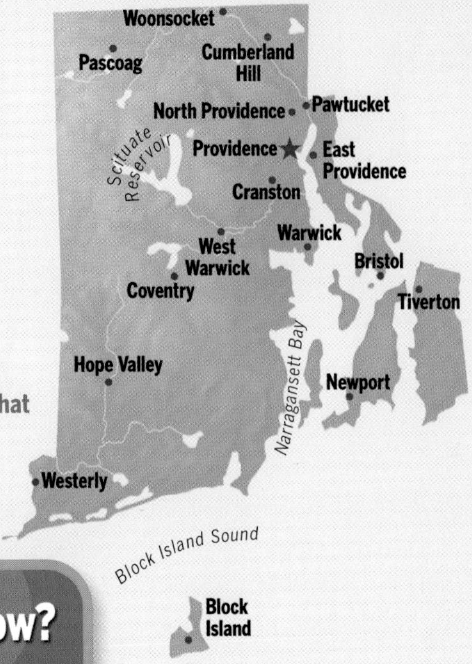

▶ Verrazano may have given the state its name when he wrote in 1524 that Block Island was about as big as the Greek "Island of Rhodes."

Block Island Sound

Block Island

Did You Know?

Rhode Island is the country's smallest state.

◀ Roger Williams served as governor of the Rhode Island colony from 1654 to 1658.

▼ Touro Synagogue, founded in Newport in 1762, is the oldest synagogue in the U.S.

Map labels: Woonsocket, Pascoag, Cumberland Hill, North Providence, Pawtucket, Providence, East Providence, Cranston, Warwick, West Warwick, Bristol, Coventry, Hope Valley, Tiverton, Newport, Westerly, Scituate Reservoir, Narragansett Bay

Earth Alert! ▶

Leatherback sea turtles are about five feet long and can weigh more than a thousand pounds.

Mystery Person ▶

Though he helped keep peace between Indians and white settlers for years, this Wampanoag leader rebelled in 1675 after three of his people were tried for murder. War between Indians and colonists raged for one year, until his death in Bristol, NH.

ANSWER: METACOMET (KING PHILIP) (1638–1676)

Vermont

14th State ★ March 4, 1791

Iroquois and Algonquian tribes lived in Vermont before European settlement. French explorer Samuel de Champlain visited the area in 1609. But Vermont's first permanent European settlement, Ft. Dummer (near today's Brattleboro), wasn't founded until 1724.

Land disputes raged in Vermont during the mid-1700s. Officials in New Hampshire and New York granted the same pieces of Vermont land to different settlers. The British government sided with the New Yorkers. But settlers with New Hampshire grants refused to give up their land. They organized themselves into a group called the Green Mountain Boys and forced out many of the New Yorkers.

During the American Revolution, the Green Mountain Boys turned their attention to fighting the British. They captured Fort Ticonderoga in 1775, and in 1777 Vermont declared itself an independent republic. Its constitution made slavery illegal. Independence lasted until

◀ Green Mountain Boys leader Ethan Allen (pointing)

▲ The state's name comes from two French words that mean "green" and "mountain:" *vert* and *mont*.

1791, when Vermont became the 14th state.

In the early 1800s, Vermont's wool industry prospered. But competition from the West caused Vermont farmers to switch from sheep to dairy farming—which is still important in the state today.

Industry never became dominant in Vermont, and the state has kept its rural character. Residents and tourists enjoy Vermont's quaint farms and villages, forested hillsides, and clear mountain streams. ★

Did You Know?
Vermont marble was used to build the U.S. Supreme Court.

▼ From a Vermont maple tree, a man collects sap for syrup.

Earth Alert! ▶
Cougars were once plentiful in Vermont. But their numbers have declined due to hunting.

Mystery Person
In 1978 this ▶ ice-cream maker and his friend Jerry Greenfield (right) opened their first "scoop shop" in an old gas station in Burlington, VT. Now there are more than 450 shops around the world. Cherry Garcia is the best-selling flavor.

ANSWER: BEN COHEN (1951)

21

Kentucky

15th *State* ★ *June 1, 1792*

▼ Kentucky is believed to come from an Indian word meaning either "land of tomorrow" or "meadowlands."

Covington
Louisville   Frankfort
Jeffersonville
Henderson   Lexington
Owensboro   Fort Knox   Richmond
Danville
Bowling Green
Hopkinsville

Cumberland Gap National Historic Park

Explorers Thomas Walker and Daniel Boone wandered across Kentucky in the late 1760s and early 1770s. British law did not allow settlement west of the Appalachian Mountains. And local Indians, such as the Shawnee and the Iroquois, resisted the newcomers. Still, Harrodsburg was established in 1774. A year later, Boone led pioneers across the Cumberland Gap to found Boonesborough.

Frequent battles between settlers and Indians—who mostly sided with the British— took place during the American Revolution. After the war settlers made their way to the fertile bluegrass valley. Louisville was founded alongside the Ohio River. Originally part of Virginia, Kentucky became a state in 1792.

Kentucky was divided on the issue of slavery. During the Civil War it supplied both

▶ Autumn in Pine Mountain State Park, southern Appalachians

Union and Confederate troops. Though it was a slaveholding state, Kentucky stayed in the Union.

Because of the mountains, eastern Kentucky was the last part of the state to be settled. Railroads didn't enter the region until the 1890s. They made it easier to harvest important resources such as lumber and coal.

Kentucky has been a center for horse breeding since the mid-1700s. Today the state has world-class horse farms. Coal has remained important in Kentucky. But the state's economy also depends on tobacco, manufacturing, and tourism. ✪

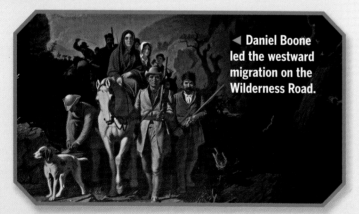

◀ Daniel Boone led the westward migration on the Wilderness Road.

Earth Alert! ▶
Price's potato-bean plant is named for Sadie Price, who collected it in Kentucky in 1896.

Mystery Person
▶ As a young man, this Kentucky native attended the United States Military Academy in West Point, NY. He later served in Congress. But during the Civil War he turned against the U.S. government—in 1862 he was elected president of the Confederacy.

ANSWER: JEFFERSON DAVIS (1808–1889)

Tennessee

16th *State* ★ *June 1, 1796*

▲ Congress created the Tennessee Valley Authority in 1933. TVA dams create electricity in seven states along the Tennessee River.

Cherokee and Chickasaw Indians inhabited Tennessee's mountains and river valleys for centuries before Europeans arrived. Hernando de Soto explored the region in 1540, and French settlement began along the banks of the Mississippi River in the early 1700s.

The British claimed the area in 1763, after the French and Indian War. Eastern Tennessee was then part of North Carolina. But after the Revolutionary War, in 1784, North Carolina gave that land to the federal government as payment for a war debt. The people who lived there did not like this, and they decided to form their own country, Franklin. It disbanded three years later. In 1790 Tennessee became a separate U.S. territory. It joined the Union in 1796.

The people of Tennessee did not agree on the issue of slavery, but the state joined the Confederacy at the start of the Civil War.

◄ Nashville, TN, is America's country music capital.

Map labels: Clarksville · Nashville · Murfreesboro · Jackson · Memphis · Savannah · Knoxville · Chattanooga · Kingsport · Johnson City · Tennessee River · Cumberland Mountains · Appalachian Mountains

▲ Tanasie, an Indian village in the area, is the origin of the state's name.

In 1862 Union forces invaded and won the Battle of Shiloh. After the war Tennessee was the first state to rejoin the Union.

Today Tennessee is an industrial state. Chemical processing, electronic machinery, and textile production are important to the state's economy. And though it is less dependent on farming than it was in the past, tobacco is Tennessee's most important crop. ✪

Did You Know?

On a clear day, seven states are visible from the top of Tennessee's Lookout Mountain.

Earth Alert! ►

Early Americans used the Tennessee purple coneflower to treat headaches and snake bites.

Mystery Person ► This Tennessee

track star won three gold medals at the 1960 Olympics. Her accomplishment earned her many fans. One of them was the mayor of Clarksville, her hometown. The parade he hosted in her honor was the town's first non-segregated event.

ANSWER: WILMA RUDOLPH (1940-1994)

23

Ohio

17th *State* ★ *March 1, 1803*

▶ Ohio is an Iroquois word meaning "great water." It probably referred to the Ohio River.

French explorer Robert Cavelier, Sieur de La Salle, was probably the first European to see Ohio, around 1670. The French and the British both claimed the area, which was home to the Iroquois Indians. But in 1763 the French lost most of their lands east of the Mississippi, including Ohio, to Britain.

After the American Revolution, in 1787, land north of the Ohio River and west of Pennsylvania became the Northwest Territory. War veterans established Marietta, the area's first permanent white settlement, a year later. But there were frequent clashes with Indians who resented the takeover of their land. After the Battle of Fallen Timbers in 1794, they were forced to give up a large part of Ohio, and more settlers arrived to farm the

◀ The Rock and Roll Hall of Fame and Museum brings visitors to Cleveland.

fertile river valleys.

Ohio became a state in 1803. And after the Civil War ended in 1865, manufacturing and coal and iron ore industries expanded rapidly. The Erie Canal, which linked Lake Erie with the Atlantic Ocean, and railroads made it easier to ship products to eastern markets. Foreign competition slowed some of Ohio's industries during the late 20th century. But Ohio remains a major Midwest industrial state, producing cars, chemicals, steel, processed food, and machinery. Tourism is also important. ✪

▼ Erie Canal, opening day (1825). DeWitt Clinton pours lake water into the Atlantic Ocean.

Did You Know?

Seven U.S. presidents were born in Ohio—James Garfield, Ulysses S. Grant, Warren G. Harding, Benjamin Harrison, Rutherford B. Hayes, William McKinley, and William Howard Taft.

Earth Alert! ▶ Lake Erie watersnakes live on islands in the western part of the lake.

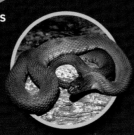

Mystery Person In 1980 this ▶ architecture student from Athens, OH, entered a contest that would change her life. She was selected to design the Vietnam Veterans Memorial in Washington, DC. Today people visit the memorial to remember the men and women who died in the war.

24

ANSWER: MAYA LIN (1959)

Louisiana

18th State ★ April 30, 1812

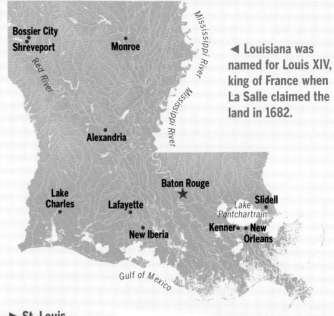

◄ Louisiana was named for Louis XIV, king of France when La Salle claimed the land in 1682.

Several Indian nations, including the Tunica and Caddo, were among Louisiana's first occupants. Spanish explorer Hernando de Soto crossed the area in 1541. But when he didn't find gold, he moved on. Then, in 1682, Robert Cavelier, Sieur de La Salle, claimed all the land for France from the Mississippi River to the Rocky Mountains. The area was called French Louisiana.

At the end of the French and Indian War, in 1763, France had to give the territory to Spain. But in 1802, Spain secretly transferred it back to France. President Thomas Jefferson did not want this powerful European nation to control land that was so close to the U.S. So in 1803 he bought it for $15 million. The Louisiana Purchase doubled the size of the young country. The U.S. carved all or part of 15 states from the territory. In 1812 land in the southern region became the state of Louisiana.

▲ Meriwether Lewis and William Clark were hired by Thomas Jefferson to explore the Louisiana Territory.

► St. Louis Cathedral, founded in New Orleans's French Quarter in 1718

Did You Know?

In 2005 New Orleans flooded as a result of Hurricane Katrina, one of our country's worst natural disasters.

Today Louisiana has one of the South's most diverse populations. The city of New Orleans has strong French, Spanish, Native American, and African roots.

Oil, gas, and chemical industries are important to the state's economy. Its warm climate, lively music, unique foods, and festivals attract tourists from around the world. ✪

Earth Alert! ►
The construction of new homes has destroyed the Louisiana black bear's natural habitat.

Mystery Person Born ►
in New Orleans, LA, and nicknamed "Satchmo," this trumpet player and singer is considered to be the father of American jazz. He toured the world and gave about 300 concerts a year. His music is still popular with fans today.

ANSWER: LOUIS ARMSTRONG (1901-1971)

25

Indiana

19th State ★ December 11, 1816

When French explorer Robert Cavelier, Sieur de La Salle, came through Indiana in 1679, Miami and Potawatomi Indians inhabited the region. More than fifty years later, in 1732, Indiana's first European settlement was established at Vincennes.

French and British businessmen competed to control the region's fur trade in the 1700s. Beaver hats were popular in Europe. Because of this, the animal's fur became valuable. After the French and Indian War in 1763, the British gained all French-held land east of the Mississippi, including Indiana. But they lost it after the American Revolution. In 1783 Indiana became part of the Northwest Territory. Conflict continued as

▼ A huge bucket of iron ore, limestone, and coke at the U.S. Steel factory, 1909

▶ The state's name may mean "land of the Indians."

Indians resisted white settlement. But American victories at Fallen Timbers (1794) and Tippecanoe (1811) pushed Indians off the land. Settlers streamed in to take advantage of the area's rich farmland. In 1816 Indiana became a state.

In the late 1800s, Indiana's industries expanded. Natural gas was discovered, and Standard Oil built a huge refinery. In 1906 U.S. Steel constructed its biggest plant. The city of Gary, Indiana, was built up around it to house the company's workers.

Agriculture is also important to the economy. Indiana farmers grow corn, wheat, and soybeans. The state is also a top poultry producer. ✪

(Map labels: Gary, South Bend, Fort Wayne, Wabash River, Lafayette, Muncie, Anderson, Indianapolis, Richmond, Terre Haute, Columbus, Bloomington, White River, Vincennes, Evansville)

Did You Know?

The first U.S. public school to teach boys and girls in the same classroom was established in New Harmony, IN, in the late 1800s.

▲ Since 1911 the Indianapolis 500, a popular auto race, has been held at the Indianapolis Motor Speedway.

Earth Alert! ▶
Pitcher's thistle grows in northern Indiana, along the sandy shore of Lake Michigan.

Mystery Person This U.S. president ▶ moved to Indiana when he was eight years old. He worked on his family's farm and rarely went to school. Instead, he taught himself. As president, he spoke out against slavery. And on January 1, 1863, he signed the Emancipation Proclamation, freeing slaves.

ANSWER: ABRAHAM LINCOLN (1809-1865)

Mississippi

20th *State* ★ *December 10, 1817*

Named after the river, Mississippi is an Indian word meaning "father of waters."

Map cities: Southaven, Holly Springs, Oxford, Tupelo, Greenville, Vicksburg, Jackson, Meridian, Natchez, Hattiesburg, Ocean Springs, Pascagoula, Gulfport, Biloxi
Rivers: Mississippi River, Pearl River

As Spanish explorer Hernando de Soto traveled Mississippi in 1541, Choctaw, Chickasaw, and other Indian groups were living in the area. France claimed Mississippi as part of the Louisiana Territory in the late 1600s and established settlements at Ocean Springs (1699) and Natchez (1716). At the end of the French and Indian War in 1763, the land came under British control. But they turned it over to the U.S. after the American Revolution.

Mississippi became a state in 1817. During the 1830s, the U.S. government forced the remaining Indians out, sending them west to Indian Territory. White settlers then used the rich land for growing cotton. Soon huge plantations worked by slaves were built across the state.

▲ In the 1800s elegant steamboats like the *Great Republic* transported passengers to cities along the Mississippi River.

Mississippi joined the Confederacy during the Civil War, and many battles were fought here. Union General Ulysses S. Grant won the decisive Battle of Vicksburg, giving the Union control of the Mississippi River.

Racial discrimination continued to be a problem after slavery ended. During the 1960s, violent clashes occurred as blacks struggled for equal rights. Since then, Mississippians have worked to put the legacy of racial conflict behind them.

Today cotton is still vital to the state's economy. But logging, fish harvesting, and industry have become increasingly important. ✪

▼ Cotton blooms on a Mississippi farm.

Earth Alert! ▶

A small group of Mississippi gopher frogs survive in the DeSoto National Forest.

Mystery Person ▶
A writer and civil rights activist, this woman was born to enslaved parents in Holly Springs, MS. She spoke out against lynching and, in 1909, co-founded the National Association for the Advancement of Colored People (NAACP).

ANSWER: IDA B. WELLS- BARNETT (1862-1931)

Illinois

21st *State* ★ *December 3, 1818*

▶ Illinois reflects the French explorers' spelling of *Iliniwek*, the name of an Indian group that lived in the area.

Map labels: Waukegan, Rockford, Elgin, Chicago, Naperville, Aurora, Cicero, Joliet, Rock Island, Peoria, Mississippi River, Illinois River, Quincy, Springfield, Decatur, Charleston, East St. Louis, Carbondale

Thousands of years ago, Illinois's first people built huge burial mounds that still dot the state. When French explorers Jacques Marquette and Louis Joliet arrived in 1673, Cahokia and Chippewa Indians populated the region.

The French set up fur trading posts and small settlements in the late 1600s and early 1700s. But the area's population did not increase until after the American Revolution. When Illinois became a state in 1818, it still did not have the required population. Congress made an exception because of the area's rich farmland and the country's desire for westward expansion. With the opening of the Erie Canal in 1825, European immigrants and settlers from the East poured into northern Illinois, eager for work.

Did You Know?

Opened in 1929, Chicago's Shedd Aquarium is one of the oldest public aquariums in the world.

▼ This man grows alfalfa, beans, oats, and corn on his Illinois farm.

Illinois stayed in the Union during the Civil War, but many people in southern Illinois sympathized with the South. After the war, industry boomed. Chicago became the nation's meatpacking and grain center. And when a fire started in a small barn in October 1871, destroying most of the city within 24 hours, the city was quickly rebuilt and modernized.

Today northern Illinois is largely urban and industrial. Chicago, its hub, is now a center for iron and steel production. Southern Illinois has many farms, and corn remains an important crop. ✪

▼ Chicago waterfront, 1913. It was then—and still is—the country's third largest city.

Earth Alert! ▶
The Hine's emerald dragonfly is named for its bright green body and eyes.

Mystery Person
In 1931 this ▶ social worker from Cedarville, IL, won the Nobel Peace Prize. But she is best known as the founder of Hull House. The organization, called a settlement house, opened in Chicago in 1889 to help immigrants and the poor. Today it is a museum.

28

Alabama

22nd *State* ★ *December 14, 1819*

Cherokee, Creek, Choctaw, and Chickasaw Indians lived in Alabama thousands of years before Spanish explorers arrived in the 1500s. They searched for gold. But it was the French who built the first permanent European settlement, today's Mobile, in 1702.

Most of the region changed hands—between the French, English, and Americans—several times during the next hundred years. After capturing Mobile during the War of 1812, the U.S. controlled all of present-day Alabama. It became a state in 1819.

Cotton plantations dominated Alabama in the early 1800s. As a slave state, Alabama withdrew from the Union in 1861, at the start of the Civil War. Seven years later it was readmitted.

Cotton remained important after the war. But deposits of coal

◄ Alabama was named after the Alabama River and a group of Indians who lived in the area. The Indian name means "people who clear the thicket."

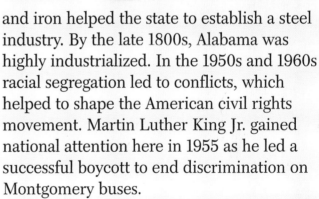

► The arrest of Rosa Parks sparked the Montgomery Bus Boycott. A year later, buses were integrated.

and iron helped the state to establish a steel industry. By the late 1800s, Alabama was highly industrialized. In the 1950s and 1960s racial segregation led to conflicts, which helped to shape the American civil rights movement. Martin Luther King Jr. gained national attention here in 1955 as he led a successful boycott to end discrimination on Montgomery buses.

Today the paper and chemical industries are important sources of jobs for Alabama residents. And one of the nation's leading medical research centers is located in Birmingham. ✪

Did You Know?

The first electric trolleys in the U.S. rolled through the streets of Montgomery in 1866.

▲ The U.S. Space and Rocket Center in Huntsville, AL, opened to the public in 1970.

Earth Alert! ►

The white-topped pitcher plant is carnivorous. Insects are easily trapped inside its tubular leaves.

Mystery Person Born into slavery, this teacher and scientist dedicated himself to improving the lives of hard-working southern farmers. At Alabama's Tuskegee Institute (now Tuskegee University) he developed ways to help them enrich their soil by growing peanuts and soybeans instead of cotton.

ANSWER: GEORGE WASHINGTON CARVER (1864–1943)

Maine

Allagash

Houlton

◄ Maine may stand for mainland, in contrast to the islands where some early settlers lived. It may also have been named for a province in France.

White Mountains

Penobscot River

Bangor

Augusta ★

Acadia National Park

Lewiston

Auburn • Brunswick

Portland

Biddeford

Sanford

Atlantic Ocean

Algonquian Indian tribes lived in Maine for thousands of years before the first European ships reached its rocky coast in the 1500s. In the 1620s, English settlers established villages along Maine's sheltered coves and on its tiny islands. These isolated settlements joined the growing Massachusetts Bay Colony in the 1650s. To encourage settlement in its northern province, colonial leaders offered free land to people willing to live in Maine. Many accepted, and the region grew quickly in the mid-1700s.

During the American Revolution, British ships attacked Maine's coastal towns. Falmouth (today's Portland) was burned. Since the Massachusetts government couldn't protect Maine during the Revolution, some Mainers decided it was time to control their own affairs. The independence movement grew, and Maine was separated from Massachusetts after the War of 1812.

▼ Fishers catch lobster along the cold-water coast.

Did You Know?

About 90 percent of Maine is covered by forest.

▲ Acadia was the first national park east of the Mississippi River.

Competition for power between free and slave states in the early 1800s influenced Maine's history. Under the Missouri Compromise, Maine entered the Union as a free state in 1820. A year later, Missouri was admitted as a slave state.

In the early 1900s, Maine's rushing rivers powered textile mills and shoe manufacturing plants. Today Maine's extensive forests provide paper and wood products, and farmers grow potatoes—Maine's most famous crop. ✪

Earth Alert! ►

Researchers track paw prints to figure out how many Canada lynx live in Maine.

Mystery Person ► This writer,

born in Rockland, ME, was one of the most popular poets of her time. Her first book of poetry was published in 1917. Another of her poetry collections earned the Pulitzer Prize. Steepletop, her New York home, is a National Historic Landmark.

ANSWER: EDNA ST. VINCENT MILLAY (1892–1950)

Missouri

24th State ★ August 10, 1821

The Osage, Missouri, and Fox Indians inhabited Missouri when the first French explorers—Jacques Marquette, Louis Joliet, and Robert Cavelier, Sieur de La Salle—traveled down the Mississippi River in the late 1600s. Missouri was part of the land La Salle claimed for France. He called the territory Louisiana. The first permanent European settlement, at Ste. Genevieve, was established around 1735. Several settlements followed, including St. Louis in 1764. Still, the area was never that important to France. When Napoleon needed money in 1803, he sold it to the United States. Missouri was one of the regions gained in the Louisiana Purchase.

In 1821 Missouri entered the Union as a slave state—to balance the admission of Maine as a free state the year before. Soon Missouri became the gateway to the frontier, with the Oregon Trail starting in Independence on its route to the west.

◀ The state takes its name from the Missouri River. Missouri may mean "town of large canoes."

▲ Pony Express riders traveled between St. Joseph, MO, and Sacramento, CA, delivering mail.

During the Civil War, Missouri stayed in the Union. Bloody battles were fought in this border state, with each side seeking control.

Farming is vitally important to present-day Missouri. Top crops include grain, hay, and soybeans. But the state's largest cities—St. Louis and Kansas City—are among the biggest transportation and industrial centers in the country. ✪

Did You Know?

Some of the strongest earthquakes to hit the U.S. happened in 1811 and 1812 around New Madrid, MO.

◀ The St. Louis Gateway Arch bridges two states—Missouri and Illinois. It is as tall as a 63-story building.

Earth Alert! ▶

It might look cute, but the spotted skunk defends itself by giving off a bad odor.

Mystery Person ▶

As manager of the New York Yankees, this Missouri-born baseball player led the team to ten pennants and helped them win five world championships in a row. In 1966 he was inducted into the Baseball Hall of Fame.

ANSWER: CASEY STENGEL (1891-1975)

Arkansas

25th State ★ June 15, 1836

Indian people known as Bluff Dwellers settled in Arkansas about 12,000 years ago. But the recorded history of the state begins in 1541 with Spanish explorer Hernando de Soto. Robert Cavelier, Sieur de La Salle, claimed the region for France in 1682. Four years later, Henri de Tonti founded the first European settlement.

The U.S. gained Arkansas as part of the 1803 Louisiana Purchase. In the 1830s the federal government forced Indians off the land, and white farmers moved in. Arkansas was admitted to the Union as a slave state in 1836. (One year later, Michigan joined the Union as a free state.) During the Civil War, Arkansas joined the Confederacy.

Cotton plantations thrived in

▲ Arkansas comes from an Indian term for the Quapaw tribe, known as the downstream people.

the rich lowlands of the Mississippi and Arkansas Rivers. But in the early 1900s, rice replaced cotton as Arkansas's most important crop. The state went through hard economic times in the early years of the 20th century because of floods and, later, drought. Jobs were scarce, and many of Arkansas's farmers had to leave the state in search of work.

Since then, Arkansas's economy has improved, with food processing and lumber production taking their place alongside agriculture. And Arkansas's natural beauty has spurred the growth of a new industry—tourism. ✪

◄ Hikers on Calico Rock, Ozark Mountains

Did You Know?

At Crater of Diamonds State Park near Murfreesboro, AR, visitors can dig for gems.

▲ Arkansas ships rice around the world.

Earth Alert! ►
They thought it was extinct, but scientists now believe the ivory-billed woodpecker might be alive in Arkansas.

Mystery Person In 1957 this ►
civil rights activist helped a group of black students enroll in Little Rock's all-white Central High School. While the governor tried to keep them out, her home became a meeting place for the students, who became known as the Little Rock Nine.

ANSWER: DAISY BATES (1914-1999)

Michigan

26th State ★ January 26, 1837

Copper Harbor
Lake Superior
Ironwood
Marquette
Menominee
Cheboygan
Lake Huron
Lake Michigan
Saginaw
Grand Rapids
Flint
Kalamazoo
Lansing
Dearborn
Detroit
Ann Arbor

◄ Michigan comes from the Chippewa word *michigana*, which means "large lake."

Potawatomi and Ojibwa Indians were living in Michigan's Upper Peninsula when French explorer Etienne Brulé arrived in 1618. Other explorers, missionaries, and fur trappers followed. Jacques Marquette established Michigan's first permanent European settlement at Sault Ste. Marie in 1668. By the 1700s, there were several French missions, forts, and farms in the region.

The British gained control of Michigan after the French and Indian War in 1763. After the American Revolution, the U.S. gained control of the land. It became part of the Northwest Territory in 1787, and a state in 1837.

Iron mines opened after statehood. With the completion of the Soo Canal in 1855, barges began to transport iron ore to steel manufacturing plants on the Great Lakes. In the late 1800s, the lumber and furniture industries grew to take advantage of Michigan's forests.

By the early 20th century, industrialists had begun automobile production in Detroit, located in Michigan's Lower Peninsula. It's still an important industry. Today most of the state's people live in the Lower Peninsula. Its farms produce apples, cherries, sugar beets, and other crops. Michigan's remote Upper Peninsula depends on mining, logging, and tourism. Much of it has remain unchanged since the first explorers and trappers passed through the region centuries ago. ✪

Did You Know?

At any spot in Michigan, you are within 85 miles of at least one of the Great Lakes.

◄ Lake Michigan's Ludington Lighthouse has been a beacon for ships since 1871.

▼ Henry Ford's modern assembly line made auto production fast and cheap. His 1914 Model T was the first car built on the line.

Earth Alert! ►

The building of roads and homes threatens the natural habitat of the Mitchell's satyr butterfly.

Mystery Person

While developing vegetarian foods for patients at the Battle Creek Sanitarium, this Michigan native accidentally invented corn flakes. The cereal was so popular that he started his own company. He business prospered, and he used his earnings to help people in need.

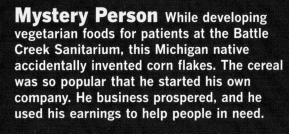

ANSWER: W. K. KELLOGG (1860–1951)

Florida

27th State ★ March 3, 1845

▲ Ponce de Leon first saw Florida a few days after Easter, which is *Pascua Florida* in Spanish. He named Florida for the holiday.

Pensacola
Tallahassee ★
Jacksonville
St. Augustine
Gainesville
Gulf of Mexico
Atlantic Ocean
John F. Kennedy Space Center
Cape Canaveral
Tampa
St. Petersburg
Sarasota
Lake Okeechobee
The Everglades
Hollywood
Hialeah
Miami
Key West

Spanish explorer Juan Ponce de León led an expedition to Florida in 1513, searching for the mythical Fountain of Youth. He didn't find it, but he claimed the land for Spain. For several years the Spanish, French, and British sought control of Florida. Then the U.S. won Florida from Spain in the Adams-Onis Treaty of 1819. At the time, Seminole Indians held some of the area's best land. To make room for European settlers, the U.S. government bought most of their land and forced those who would not sell to move west to Indian Territory. In 1845 Florida was admitted to the Union as a slave state. It joined the Confederacy at the start of the Civil War and rejoined the Union in 1868.

◄ All space shuttle flights originate at Florida's Kennedy Space Center.

▲ Castillo de San Marcos was built by the Spanish between 1672 and 1695 to defend St. Augustine. The fort still stands today.

Florida developed quickly after the war. Henry Flagler and Henry Plant built railroad lines that opened up land as far south as Miami. Swamps, including the Everglades, were drained. Farmers planted citrus trees. Resort cities grew along the coast. Tourists and new residents poured into the state.

In recent decades south Florida has become home to many Latin Americans and people from the Caribbean. Tourism is important to Florida's economy. So is agriculture—the state grows about 70 percent of the country's oranges and grapefruit. ✪

Did You Know?

Founded in 1565, St. Augustine, FL, is the oldest city in the U.S.

Earth Alert! ▶

Florida is the only state with American crocodiles. The reclusive reptiles are rarely seen by humans.

Mystery Person
In 1884 this Sarasota resident and his five brothers started a world-famous circus. Two decades later they bought London's Barnum & Bailey circus. Today his Florida home is open to visitors. The museum he founded with his wife displays his personal art collection.

ANSWER: JOHN RINGLING (1866-1936)

Texas

28th *State* ★ *December 29, 1845*

▶ The state's name comes from the word *tejas*, an Indian word meaning "friends."

Amarillo

Red River

Fort Worth • • Dallas • Atlanta
Abilene • Arlington
• Midland

• El Paso

Colorado River Austin ★

Beaumont

Rio Grande

Houston

San Antonio

Corpus Christi •

Gulf of Mexico

Caddo Indians lived in Texas when Spanish explorer Alvar Nuñez Cabeza de Vaca arrived in the 1500s. By the early 1700s, the Spanish had built forts and religious settlements, called missions, in the area. It was the northern frontier of New Spain, which included Mexico.

Mexico won its independence from Spain in 1821. That same year, Stephen Austin led 300 American families to the Texas region. Others followed, attracted by the fertile soil. The Mexican government forbade American immigration in 1830, but settlers continued to come.

In 1834 Antonio López de Santa Anna overthrew the Mexican government in Texas. American settlers rebelled and captured the town of San Antonio in 1835. Santa Anna cornered and killed a group of them at the Alamo. One year later, American forces under Sam Houston captured Santa Anna and destroyed his army. They made Texas an independent

▼ Oil field, Burkburnett, TX, 1919

Did You Know?

Texas is the nation's biggest producer of oil, cattle, sheep, minerals, and cotton.

republic. After nine years, Texas became a state in 1845.

In the late 1800s railroads helped ranchers and farmers move to remote areas of Texas. The discovery of oil near Beaumont in 1901 began an oil boom. After World War II, the aerospace and electronics industries expanded. Today Texas is a modern, industrial state with a huge and diverse population. ✪

▲ Children in San Antonio celebrate *Cinco de Mayo*, a Mexican holiday.

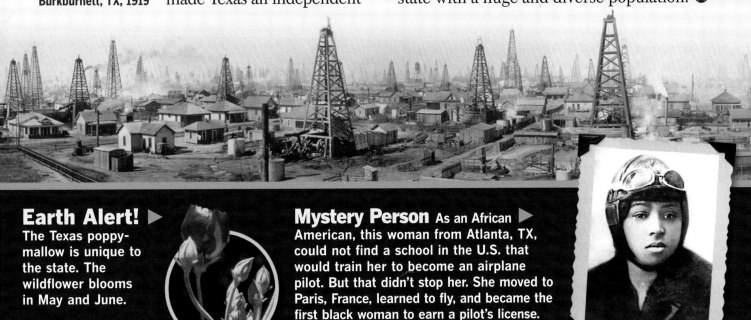

Earth Alert! ▶
The Texas poppy-mallow is unique to the state. The wildflower blooms in May and June.

Mystery Person ▶
As an African American, this woman from Atlanta, TX, could not find a school in the U.S. that would train her to become an airplane pilot. But that didn't stop her. She moved to Paris, France, learned to fly, and became the first black woman to earn a pilot's license.

ANSWER: BESSIE COLEMAN (1893-1926)

35

Iowa

29th *State* ★ *December 28, 1846*

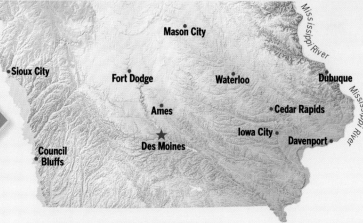

▲ The state is named for the Ioway Indians, who once lived there.

▲ Since 1911, a Butter Cow has been featured at the Iowa State Fair.

Prehistoric Indians called Mound Builders were Iowa's first inhabitants. By the time French explorers Jacques Marquette and Louis Joliet arrived in 1673, groups such as the Illinois, Miami, Sioux, and Omaha had replaced the earliest people.

Once part of French Louisiana, Iowa became U.S. land in 1803 when Thomas Jefferson bought the territory from France. During the first few decades after the Louisiana Purchase, the region was not open to white settlement. But by the 1830s settlers in Illinois were pushing the Sauk and Fox Indians west. So a strip of land in Iowa was set aside for them along the west bank of the Mississippi River. War broke out when the Indians refused to move to this set-aside region.

An 1833 treaty with the U.S. government opened the Indian lands to white settlement. People poured in, eager to take advantage of Iowa's rich farmland. In 1846 Iowa became a state. And by 1851 all Indian lands had been given to the U.S. government.

Today Iowa has some of the most fertile soil in the world. Farms cover about 90 percent of the state. Although there are fewer farms than in past decades, agriculture and businesses connected with farming employ the greatest number of Iowa residents. ✪

Did You Know?

There are about five hogs for every person in Iowa.

Earth Alert! ▶
Companies in Iowa and Wisconsin are helping peregrine falcons by building safe places for them to nest.

Mystery Person The U.S. stock ▶ market crashed during this president's first year in office. It was the start of the Great Depression. Many Americans lost their jobs and their homes. They blamed the Iowa-born president. A makeshift village of people living in poor conditions came to be called a Hooverville.

ANSWER: HERBERT HOOVER (1874–1964)

Wisconsin

30th *State* ★ *May 29, 1848*

Winnebago Indians farmed, hunted, and fished in Wisconsin when French explorer Jean Nicolet arrived in the early 1600s. Fur trappers and missionaries followed. Wisconsin became British soil in 1763, at the end of the French and Indian War. After the American Revolution the land became part of the U.S.

Large numbers of people came to Wisconsin in the 1820s when rich lead deposits were discovered in the southwest. (Because some of the miners lived in shelters dug into the hills, people called them badgers.) People from the eastern U.S. settled in the area after traveling to nearby Illinois along the Erie Canal. By 1836 Wisconsin had become a U.S. territory. It gained statehood in 1848. One of the most important political movements in U.S. history,

Progressivism, began in Wisconsin in the late 1890s and early 1900s. Progressives passed laws that regulated businesses, gave more power to ordinary people, and protected workers. Many of these reforms later spread to other states and the national government.

Most of the people of Wisconsin work in services and industry. But the state is also a leader in the production of dairy products. Herds of cows grazing in green, grassy fields are still an important symbol of the Badger State. ✪

Did You Know?

Wisconsin has more milk cows (1,500,000) than any other state.

▲ Wisconsin is an Indian word. Its meaning is uncertain, but possibilities include "homeland" and "place where wild rice grows."

◄ A Green Bay Packer football fan is called a cheesehead.

◄ Milwaukee is Wisconsin's largest city.

Map labels: Lake Superior, Superior, Lac du Flambeau, River Falls, Eau Claire, Green Bay, Lake Winnebago, Oshkosh, Mississippi River, La Crosse, Lake Michigan, Milwaukee, Madison, Waukesha, Racine, Kenosha

---

Earth Alert! ► Fasset's locoweed is probably a 10,000-year-old plant species. Wisconsin is the only place it has ever been found.

Mystery Person In 1920 the 19th ► Amendment to the Constitution gave women the right to vote. This Wisconsin woman helped make it happen. She dedicated thirty years of her life to the cause. In 1890 she joined the National American Woman Suffrage Association. Ten years later she became its president.

ANSWER: CARRIE CHAPMAN CATT (1859-1947)

California

31st State ★ September 9, 1850

Redwood National Park
• Eureka

Lake Tahoe

Sacramento ★

San Francisco • Oakland
• San Jose

• Monterey   • Fresno

• Bakersfield

Pasadena
Los Angeles •

San Diego •

Mojave Desert

Colorado River

▶ The origin of the name is uncertain, but California is thought to be the name of a fictional island paradise.

When Spanish explorer Juan Cabrillo traveled the California coast in 1542, the area was home to Cahuilla Indians. Still, he claimed the land for Spain. It remained an isolated frontier with little settlement until 1769, when the Spanish set up a series of forts and missions.

After Mexican independence from Spain in 1821, California became a Mexican province. Tales of California's fertile soil and mild climate filtered east to the U.S., and settlers began heading west in growing numbers. The U.S. offered to buy California from Mexico, but it did not become American territory until 1848 after the Mexican-American War.

The discovery of gold at Sutter's Mill in 1849 drew thousands of newcomers. After statehood was achieved in 1850, California's population continued to expand. The Pony Express, the telegraph, and the first transcontinental railroad—built largely by Chinese immigrants—linked California with the rest of the nation in the 1860s.

The early 1900s saw the growth of a new industry: moviemaking. Manufacturing and agriculture also grew in importance. Irrigation pipelines brought water from the wet northern part of the state to the fast-growing drier southern part.

Today California has the nation's largest population. Balancing growth with preservation of the land is a constant challenge. ✪

▲ Panning for gold in California's Sacramento River, 1850s

▼ San Francisco began cable car service in 1873.

Minnesota

32nd *State* ★ *May 11, 1858*

◄ The state's name comes from the Dakota word *minisota,* which means "sky-tinted waters."

Ojibwa and Sioux Indians lived in Minnesota when French explorers, fur traders, and missionaries, such as Jacques Marquette, arrived in the late 1600s. Still, France claimed the area as part of French Louisiana.

President Jefferson bought the land from France in 1803 as part of the Louisiana Purchase. The region was remote, but settlers from New England and Canada trickled in to plant crops and log the forests.

Minnesota became a U.S. territory in 1849. At the time, there were few people in the area. When the U.S. government forced Indians to give up land in southern Minnesota, however, farmers came to work the thick prairie soil.

In 1858 Minnesota became a state. Eager to increase population, the Minnesota

Did You Know?

Minnesota is called the "Land of 10,000 Lakes," but it actually has more than 11,000.

▲ Of the five Great Lakes, Lake Superior is the coldest.

government advertised in northern Europe for settlers. In 1862 the U.S. Congress passed the Homestead Act, which promised free land to settlers. Soon people from Norway, Sweden, Germany, and Denmark began to arrive. Many of today's Minnesotans are descendants of these immigrants.

Mining and manufacturing continue to be important to the state's economy. Industries such as electronics and food processing, services such as banking and insurance, and farming employ many people. Tourists are drawn to the state's sparkling lakes and deep forests. ✪

▲ By 1910 Swedish immigrants were the largest ethnic group in Minneapolis.

Earth Alert! ►
The nodding wild onion is native to Minnesota. Its fragrant leaves can be used to flavor soups.

Mystery Person Patients ►
and co-workers knew him as "Dr. Charlie." In 1914 he and his brother, Will (right), founded the Mayo Clinic in Rochester, MN. Since opening, the hospital has treated more than six million patients.

(ANSWER: CHARLES H. MAYO (1865-1939))

Oregon

33rd *State* ★ *February 14, 1859*

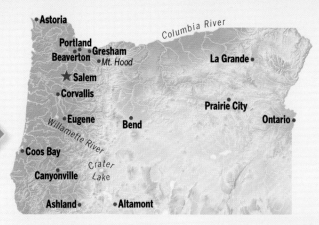

▲ The state's name comes from the Columbia River, which was once called the River Ouragon or Oregon.

In the 1500s Spanish and British explorers were the first Europeans to see Oregon. American Captain John Gray reached the Columbia River in 1792. At the time, Tillamook Indians were living in the region.

In the early 1800s Oregon Country stretched from Alaska south to California. Several nations claimed it. All but the U.S. and Britain gave up claims by the 1820s. An agreement allowed settlers and traders from the two nations into the region.

The fur trade drew many of Oregon's first white settlers. John Jacob Astor established the Astoria trading post in 1811. It was the first American settlement west of the Rocky Mountains. Settlers crossed North America in covered wagons in 1843, traveling thousands of miles along the Oregon Trail to settle in the fertile Willamette Valley.

In 1846 Britain and the U.S. split the region (the land the British kept is now part of Canada), and the Donation Land Act of 1850 increased settlement. It gave free land to white males who agreed to come to Oregon to farm. Nine years later, Oregon became the 33rd state.

Today Oregon's forests produce much of the nation's wood products. Farmers raise wheat and livestock. And Oregon's natural beauty attracts vacationers. ✪

Did You Know?

At 1,932 feet, Oregon's Crater Lake is the deepest lake in the U.S.

▲ Mount Hood, a dormant volcano outside Portland, is Oregon's highest peak.

▼ Astoria, OR, 1914. This port city still thrives today.

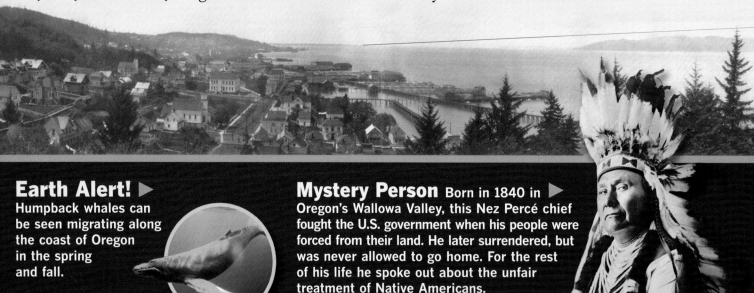

Earth Alert! ▶
Humpback whales can be seen migrating along the coast of Oregon in the spring and fall.

Mystery Person ▶
Born in 1840 in Oregon's Wallowa Valley, this Nez Percé chief fought the U.S. government when his people were forced from their land. He later surrendered, but was never allowed to go home. For the rest of his life he spoke out about the unfair treatment of Native Americans.

ANSWER: CHIEF JOSEPH (1840-1904)

Kansas

34th State ★ January 29, 1961

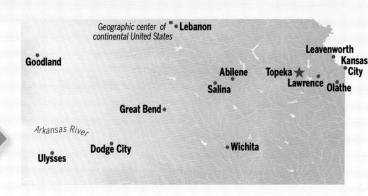

Geographic center of ●●Lebanon
continental United States

Goodland●

Leavenworth
●●Kansas
City

Abilene● Topeka ★
Salina● Lawrence● Olathe

Great Bend●

Arkansas River

Dodge City● ●Wichita

Ulysses●

▲ Named for the Kansa Indians, Kansas means "people of the south wind."

The recorded history of Kansas began when Spanish explorer Francisco de Coronado crossed its grassy plains in 1541. Pawnee and Kansa (now Kaw) Indians inhabited the region. With the 1803 Louisiana Purchase it became U.S. territory.

Starting in the 1830s, the government used Kansas to temporarily settle Indians whom it had pushed off their native lands farther east. In 1854 the Kansas-Nebraska Act opened these territories to whites. When several southern states left the Union in 1861, at the start of the Civil War, anti-slavery members of Congress finally had the power to make Kansas a slave-free state.

Between 1866 and 1885, cowboys drove herds of cattle from Texas to Kansas railroad towns such as Dodge City, Abilene, and Wichita. The cattle were then moved east on the trains. But the cowboys—weary from the trail and looking for fun—often hung around

▶ Buffalo roam free in the Tallgrass Prairie National Preserve in eastern Kansas.

▼ Dodge City, KS (seen here in 1878), has been restored. It's now a popular tourist destination.

Did You Know?
Kansas produces more wheat than any other state.

getting into trouble. Lawmen such as Wyatt Earp, "Bat" Masterson, and "Wild Bill" Hickok are famous for establishing order.

Kansas plains now grow wheat instead of wild grasses. In Wichita factories produce planes. There are still cowboys in Kansas, but they drive trucks as often as they ride horses in the wide-open spaces that are still an important part of the state's character. ✪

Earth Alert! ▶
With a height of nearly five feet, whooping cranes are the tallest birds in North America.

Mystery Person
In 1920 Prohibition made alcohol illegal in the U.S. But Kansas had banned it in 1880. When illegal saloons began cropping up in the state, this woman took matters into her own hands, destroying them with a hatchet. Her actions made her a prominent figure in the temperance movement.

ANSWER: CARRY NATION (1846–1911)

West Virginia

35th State ★ June 20, 1863

▼ West Virginia's name points to the fact that the state was formed from the western counties of Virginia.

Wheeling

Ohio River

Morgantown

Martinsburg

Parkersburg

Clarksburg

Ohio River

Elizabeth

Buckhannon *Elkins*

South Branch Potomac River

Huntington ★ *Charleston*

Kanawha River

Allegheny Mountains

White Sulphur Springs

Bluefield

West Virginia was originally part of Virginia, which became a state in 1788. The first settlers crossed the Appalachian Mountains into the region in the 1700s, where they joined Indian tribes such as the Iroquois and Shawnee.

From the start, there were important differences within Virginia. Wealthy plantation owners with enslaved blacks dominated the east. The mountainous west was an area of small family farms. At the start of the Civil War, Virginia seceded. But 40 western counties opposed this action. They set up their own government at Wheeling in 1861 to support the Union. In 1863 they joined the Union as the state of West Virginia.

▼ West Virginia coal miners, 1908

The building of railroads in the late 1800s boosted industries

Did You Know?
West Virginia has the highest average elevation of any state east of the Mississippi River.

▲ Blackwater Falls State Park

based on West Virginia's resources—coal, oil, and gas. Violent clashes occurred in the late 1800s and early 1900s between mine owners and workers struggling for better conditions, higher pay, and the right to join unions.

New energy sources reduced the demand for coal after World War II and machines cut jobs for miners. Many people left the state in search of work. Today there are even fewer jobs in the mines. But West Virginia is looking to industrial growth and tourism to provide new opportunities for its people. ✪

Earth Alert! ▶
Cheat Mountain salamanders live in the yellow birch and red spruce forests of West Virginia.

Mystery Person ▶
This Confederate general was born in Clarksburg, WV, in 1824. During the Civil War, he earned the nickname "Stonewall" for his show of strength during the Battle of Manassas. In 1863 he was accidentally fired upon by his troops and died soon after.

ANSWER: THOMAS "STONEWALL" JACKSON (1824–1863)

Nevada

36th *State* ★ *October 21, 1864*

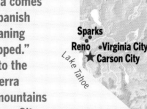

► Nevada comes from a Spanish word meaning "snowcapped." It refers to the snowy Sierra Nevada mountains near Carson City.

ntil the early 1800s, tribes including the Paiute, Shoshone, and Washoe had Nevada to themselves. European and American explorers and traders, such as Jedediah Smith, entered the region in the 1820s, looking for new sources of furs. Settlers passed through on their way to California during the 1830s and 1840s. But this dry and empty land was not a destination for most people. That changed in 1859 with the discovery of a huge silver deposit—the Comstock Lode. Prospectors poured in, making a boomtown of the nearby mining camp at Virginia City.

During the Civil War, President Lincoln pushed for Nevada statehood. He knew that many of Nevada's people were against slavery. Its voters would probably send anti-slavery senators to Congress, providing support for the Union cause. Although it didn't have the required population, Nevada became a state in 1864.

Did You Know?

◄ Nevada's state tree, the bristlecone pine, is one of the oldest trees in the world. Those in Great Basin National Park are more than 4,000 years old.

Today mining is still important in Nevada. The state is a leader in production of gold, silver, and mercury. Cattle ranches and irrigated farms dot the plains and hills. But Nevada's biggest industry is tourism. Reno and Las Vegas attract visitors from around the world, and the beauty of Nevada's deserts and mountains draws thousands of nature lovers every year. ✪

▼ In 2004 Las Vegas welcomed more than 37 million tourists.

Earth Alert! ►
Nevada is the only place in the world with steamboat buckwheat. It grows near hot springs.

Mystery Person
She was the first ► Native American woman to publish a book, *Life Among the Paiutes* (1883). Earlier, she worked in Oregon as an interpreter for the Bureau of Indian Affairs. In 1880 she met with President Rutherford B. Hayes in hopes of improving conditions on Indian reservations.

ANSWER: SARAH WINNEMUCCA HOPKINS (1844–1891)

Nebraska

37th *State* ★ *March 1, 1867*

◄ A Nebraska rancher with a herd of cattle

Several Indian groups lived in Nebraska before white settlement, including the Missouri, Omaha, Pawnee, and Dakota. Spain claimed the area in 1541. The French did the same in 1682. Neither nation settled it. But in 1803 the Louisiana Purchase made the region part of the U.S.

The area's first permanent settlement, Bellevue, was established in 1823 along the Missouri River. Still, most of the people who entered Nebraska didn't stay. Pioneers passed through as they followed the Oregon Trail to the west. Some called Nebraska's dry plains the "Great American Desert" and wrote that it was not fit for farming. Seeing little value in Nebraska, the federal government made it Indian Territory for the first half of the 1800s. White settlement was forbidden.

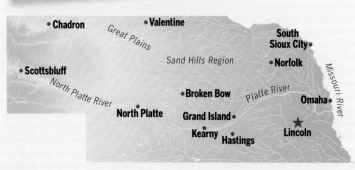
• Chadron · Great Plains · Valentine · South Sioux City · Sand Hills Region · Norfolk · Scottsbluff · North Platte River · Broken Bow · Platte River · Omaha · Missouri River · North Platte · Grand Island · Kearny · Hastings · Lincoln

▲ *Nebrathka,* an Indian word meaning "flat water," refers to the Platte River, which flows over Nebraska's plains.

In 1854 the U.S. government changed its view. It forced Indians out and opened Nebraska to whites. The 1862 Homestead Act gave each settler 160 acres of land. New railroads brought even more people. In 1867 Nebraska became a state.

Farming expanded in Nebraska in the 1890s with irrigation. Now Nebraska contains some of the country's most productive farmland. Fields of corn and soybeans are common in the eastern part of the state, while wheat and cattle dominate the drier western counties. ✪

▼ In 1888 this Civil War veteran and his family moved to Nebraska to start a new life.

Did You Know?

Many Nebraska homesteaders lived in sod houses, or soddies, which were made from the thick, grass-covered surface of the ground.

Earth Alert! ►

Piping plovers nest along Nebraska's Platte River. They lay their eggs in the sand.

Mystery Person ►

Born in Omaha, NE, this African American leader spoke out about injustice. Both he and Martin Luther King Jr. wanted equality for blacks, but they had different ideas about how to achieve their goals.

ANSWER: MALCOLM X (EL HAJJ MALIK EL-SHABAZZ) (1925-1965)

Colorado

38th State ★ August 1, 1876

▲ The Spanish called the area *Colorado*, meaning "red," because of its red-rock canyons and soil.

Arapaho and Cheyenne Indians roamed eastern Colorado long before Spanish explorers arrived in the 1600s. Both the Spanish and French claimed the area at different times. In 1803 the U.S. purchased part of eastern Colorado—Louisiana Territory—from France.

But the mountainous west was still controlled by Spain. It became part of Mexico in 1821. But after losing the Mexican-American War in 1848, Mexico had to give it to the U.S.

Large groups of settlers reached Colorado in the late 1850s when gold was discovered near present-day Denver. Growth driven by mining helped Colorado become a state in 1876. Soon after, a silver-mining boom brought even more people.

Water has also been important to Colorado's growth. Its dry eastern plains needed irrigation to become rich farmland. Farm production increased in the late 1800s, with sugar beets as the main crop. By the early 1900s, farming surpassed mining as the state's main industry. Since then, the government has built dams and pipelines to bring in water from the Rocky Mountains.

In recent years, tourism has become important to the state's economy. Aspen and Vail are popular ski resorts. The state also produces coal, oil, and gas. Beautiful scenery and resource wealth continue to help Colorado grow at a rapid pace. ★

▲ Pueblo Indian cliff dwellings in Mesa Verde National Park

▼ Rocky Mountain skyline, Denver, CO, 1898

Did You Know?

Denver, CO, is known as the Mile High City because it is exactly one mile (5,280 feet) above sea level.

Earth Alert! ▶
Biologists have established black-footed ferret colonies in Colorado's Coyote Basin and at Wolf Creek.

Mystery Person This Colorado woman was on board the *Titanic* when it sank in 1912. She helped row a lifeboat to safety and became a national hero when she organized wealthy passengers to donate money to those who had lost everything. People said she was "unsinkable." ▶

(ANSWER: MOLLY BROWN (1867–1932))

North Dakota

39th *State* ★ *November 2, 1889*

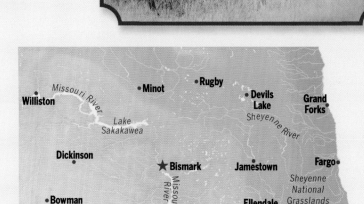
▼ North Dakota farmers gather around a steam-powered tractor, early 1900s.

When French Canadian explorers crossed North Dakota in the 1730s, they found Mandan, Hidatsa, and Lakota Sioux Indians. France had already claimed much of the area in 1682 but didn't settle it. In 1803 France sold this land to the United States as part of the Louisiana Purchase.

The U.S. government encouraged homesteaders to move to Dakota Territory in the 1860s. But it was hard to reach, and ongoing wars with Indians scared many whites. When the Northern Pacific Railway crossed the area in the 1870s, settlement picked up. By this time local Indian tribes had been weakened by battles with the U.S. Army. And their primary food source, bison, had been hunted almost to extinction. When the Sioux surrendered in 1881, the peace that followed made the area more attractive to settlers.

The Dakota Territory was split into north and south sections in February

▲ Dakota is the name of a group of Indians who lived in the area. They are also called Lakota Sioux.

Did You Know?

The town of Rugby is the geographical center of North America.

1889. That November, North Dakota became the 39th state. Farming expanded in the early 1900s, and the state passed laws to ease economic burdens on farmers and rural families.

Today most North Dakotans farm or have jobs connected to agriculture. They continue to plow and plant the state's rich soil much as the first homesteaders did almost 150 years ago. ✪

◄ North Dakota's annual sunflower harvest is enough to fill 415 million bags of sunflower seeds.

Earth Alert! ▶

Western prairie fringed orchids can be found in the Sheyenne National Grasslands in southeastern North Dakota.

Mystery Person ▶

When American forces tried to take over sacred land, this Lakota Sioux chief fought back. The Battle of Little Big Horn took place in 1874. General Custer and his army were defeated. Still, the U.S. government made the Indians move. Gold had been found on their land.

ANSWER: SITTING BULL (1831–1890)

South Dakota

40th *State* ★ *November 2, 1889*

▲ Mount Rushmore honors four U.S. presidents.

Before white settlers arrived, South Dakota was home to Cheyenne and Arikara Indians. The Lakota Sioux joined them in the 1700s, when white settlers pushed them west from Minnesota.

The first Europeans to travel through South Dakota, the La Vérendrye brothers, claimed the land for France. South Dakota became American soil when the U.S. bought French Louisiana in 1803. The first permanent settlement, Fort Pierre, was founded in 1817.

In the early 1800s, most South Dakota settlers were connected with the fur trade and lived along the Missouri River. But land disputes with the Sioux caused frequent fighting. A treaty gave the Indians most of the region west of the river and brought peace for a while. But whites violated the agreement

▲ *Dakota* is an Indian word that means "allies" or "friends."

when gold was discovered in the Black Hills in the 1870s. Prospectors poured into the Indians' sacred land.

In 1889 Dakota Territory was divided into north and south. Soon after, North and South Dakota entered the Union. The following year hundreds of Sioux were killed near Wounded Knee. The state opened more Indian land to white settlement and distributed it by lottery.

Today tourism is a billion-dollar business in South Dakota, but farming and agriculture remain important to the state's economy. ✪

Did You Know?

South Dakota is home to the nation's largest bison herd.

▼ Sioux men and women on South Dakota's Pine Ridge Reservation, 1891

Earth Alert! ▶

With its shovel-like nose and long tail, some people think the pallid sturgeon looks like a dinosaur.

Mystery Person ▶ Five of this

writer's books take place in South Dakota. Her first, *Little House in the Big Woods*, was published in 1935. Today her stories about life on the prairie are still popular. Visitors to DeSmet, SD, can tour one of the author's old homes.

ANSWER: LAURA INGALLS WILDER (1867–1957)

47

Montana

41st *State* ★ *November 8, 1889*

▲ Glacier National Park has more than 700 miles of hiking trails.

Many Indian nations occupied Montana before European trappers crossed its plains and mountains in the early 1700s. But Montana's history as a part of the U.S. began in 1803, with the Louisiana Purchase. Hired by the federal government to survey the new territory, a team led by Meriwether Lewis and William Clark were the first Americans to see it. A few fur traders and missionaries ventured to this remote land in the early 1800s. But large numbers of people didn't come until gold was discovered in 1852.

Montana became a U.S. territory in 1864, mainly because of the need to bring law and order to the mining camps. As settlers moved into Montana, conflicts between the U.S. Army and Indians became more frequent. In 1876 the Sioux and Cheyenne killed Lt. Colonel George Custer and more than two hundred of his men in a famous battle near the Little Bighorn River.

During the 1880s railroads crossed Montana and the territory became a state in 1889. Cattle and sheep ranchers looking for inexpensive land arrived throughout the early 1900s.

Today the state's clean air, beautiful scenery, and wide-open spaces attract many visitors. Ski resorts, parks, and historic areas now allow people to use the state's resources in a way that also preserves them. ✪

▼ George Armstrong Custer was an officer in the Civil War.

▲ Montana is based on a word that means "mountainous" in Spanish.

Did You Know?

Montana has more species of mammals than any other state.

Map labels: Glacier National Park, Kalispell, Flat Head Lake, Missoula, Dillon, Shelby, Great Falls, Helena, Bozeman, Havre, Milk River, Missouri River, Lewistown, Billings, Hardin, Wolf Point, Fort Peck Lake, Yellowstone River, Baker

Earth Alert! ▶

Researchers in Montana's northwestern Rocky Mountains use a technique called hair snagging to track grizzly bears.

Mystery Person
Born in Missoula, MT, ▶ this peace activist was the first woman elected to the U.S. Congress. She served from 1914 to 1916 and, later, from 1941 to 1943. She was the only Congress member to vote against entering World War II. A statue of her is on display in the U.S. Capitol.

ANSWER: JEANETTE RANKIN (1880-1973)

Washington

42nd State ★ November 11, 1889

Before Spanish and English explorers sailed along its coast in the 1500s, Washington was home to Indian tribes such as the Cayuse, Nez Percé, and Yakima. Several expeditions passed through in the early 1800s, looking for the Northwest Passage, a water route from the Atlantic to the Pacific. It was never discovered, but the area's rich animal life attracted American and British fur trappers and traders.

Both the U.S. and Britain claimed Washington in the early 1800s. At the time, the land was part of Oregon Territory. In 1846 the two countries agreed on how to divide the land. And in 1853 Congress created Washington Territory out of the northern part of Oregon Territory.

Settlement increased in the 1860s when gold was discovered near Walla Walla. The Northern Pacific Railroad, which connected the region to the East in 1883, also spurred population growth. Washington became a state in 1889. By that time, agriculture was booming in the fertile valleys.

Today Washington's snow-capped mountains and lush forests attract tourists. Its eastern farmlands produce wheat—and more apples and pears than any other state. The state's largest city, Seattle, is a center for high-tech industry. ✪

▲ The state was named for George Washington, the nation's first president.

▲ The Seattle Space Needle opened in 1962.

◄ American frontiersman and fur trapper Jim Bridger

Idaho

43rd State ★ July 3, 1890

The United States acquired Idaho as part of the Louisiana Purchase in 1803. The first whites to see Idaho were members of the Lewis and Clark expedition, who were sent west by President Thomas Jefferson to explore the land. In the years that followed, a few trading posts were established. When gold was discovered in the 1860s, a wave of miners and settlers followed.

This new settlement sparked conflicts with local Indian tribes such as the Nez Percé and the Bannock, who were being pushed off their land. Some tribes staged violent rebellions, and many were forced to live on reservations. When railroads entered the region in the 1880s and 1890s, they paved the way for further settlement by whites.

After Idaho became a state in 1890, the federal government built dams and canals that brought water from the Snake River to Idaho's rich but dry soils. Farm acreage increased. After World War II, the manufacturing and food processing industries also grew, and people from rural areas moved to cities, such as Boise, for jobs.

In recent decades Boise has become the headquarters for several large computer, timber, and food processing companies. As the state grows, its rich soil, abundant forests, and minerals continue to be important for its future. ✪

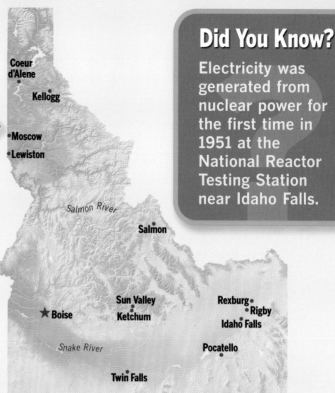

Did You Know?

Electricity was generated from nuclear power for the first time in 1951 at the National Reactor Testing Station near Idaho Falls.

▲ Idaho was the name of both a steamship that sailed the Columbia River and a gold mine.

▼ Idaho is famous for its potatoes.

▼ Tourists enjoy paddle rafting on the Salmon River.

Earth Alert! ▶

The clearing of Idaho's forests has caused the woodland caribou population to decline.

Mystery Person

This farm boy from Rigby, ID, first sketched his idea for transmitting light by electrons, one line at a time, on a blackboard for his high school science teacher. Six years later, at the age of 21, he successfully demonstrated his invention: the electronic television.

ANSWER: PHILO T. FARNSWORTH (1906–1971)

Wyoming

44th *State* ★ *July 10, 1890*

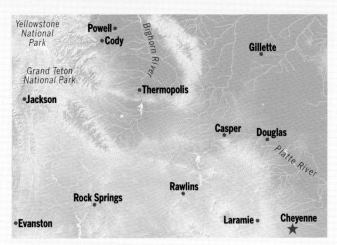

▲ *Wyoming* is an Indian word that means "on the great plains."

Arapaho, Cheyenne, and other Indian tribes have inhabited Wyoming's expansive lands for thousands of years. But white settlement occurred only two hundred years ago. Much of Wyoming became U.S. territory with the 1803 Louisiana Purchase. Soon after, American fur trappers and traders established trading posts that became important towns, such as Laramie.

During the mid-1800s, several of the most important trails to the west—the Oregon Trail, the California Trail, and the Mormon Trail—cut across the region. Thousands of settlers came through. But few chose to stay on Wyoming's dry, eastern plains or in its high mountains.

In the late 1800s, several events increased Wyoming's population. Gold was discovered, and railroad lines were built across the state. Cattle ranching began. People were also attracted to the natural beauty of Yellowstone, the first U.S. national park, created by

Did You Know?

In 1869 Wyoming women became the first in the world to be given the right to vote.

President Theodore Roosevelt in 1872. In 1890 Wyoming became the 44th state.

In the 20th century, irrigation projects brought power and water to isolated towns and farms. Oil, uranium, and coal provided needed resources—and jobs. Wyoming has few people and a harsh environment. But that environment has attracted tourists that support the state's economy. Its vast plains, rugged mountains, rodeos, and ranches provide people with a taste of the Old West. ✪

▲ A geyser shoots hot water in Yellowstone National Park.

◄ Pioneers traveled through Wyoming in horse-drawn covered wagons.

Earth Alert! ►
The Cheyenne Mountain Zoo is helping to breed endangered Wyoming toads.

Mystery Person ►
Her husband was governor of Wyoming, but when he died she was elected to complete his term in office. She was the first female governor in the U.S. She continued to be involved in government until her death at the age of 101. She is buried in Cheyenne.

ANSWER: NELLIE TAYLOE ROSS (1876–1977)

Utah

45th State ★ January 4, 1896

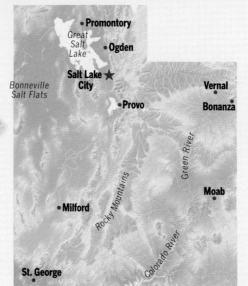

◄ Utah takes its name from the Ute Indians, who lived in the area at the time of white settlement.

When Spanish explorers Silvestre Vélez de Escalante and Francisco Atanasio Domínguez arrived in the late 1700s, the Ute, Paiute, and Shoshone were living in Utah. A religious group called the Mormons established the first permanent white settlements in the area in 1847. They set up farms and used irrigation to grow crops in the dry climate. At the time, the land was part of Mexico, but it became U.S. territory in 1848 after the Mexican-American War.

The Mormons applied for statehood in 1850 and again in 1856, but the U.S. Congress rejected the bids due to the group's practice of polygamy, or multiple marriages. Meanwhile, settlement expanded throughout the area around the Great Salt Lake, in the Wasatch Mountains. Finally, in 1896, Utah became a state.

In the early 1900s the U.S. government helped build irrigation projects, which opened up more farmland. Transportation networks grew, giving farms and mines better access to markets. Gold and silver mines in the Bingham Canyon increased production, as did copper and coal mines.

Today Utah is still rich in natural resources. But high-tech industry such as the production of computer hardware and software is also important. So is tourism. The state's snow-capped mountains, deep canyons, and colorful mesas attract people from around the world. ✪

Did You Know?

Utah's Great Salt Lake is three to five times saltier than ocean water; fish can't survive in it, but the tiny brine shrimp thrives.

◄ The state capitol overlooks Salt Lake City.

▼ Promontory, UT, 1869. Workers celebrate the completion of the transcontinental railroad.

Earth Alert! ►

Ten years after the Endangered Species Act was passed, the number of Utah prairie dogs nearly tripled.

Mystery Person ►

He became president of the Mormon Church in 1847. Earlier that year, he led his followers to Salt Lake City, UT. There he hoped they would be able to practice their religion freely. He encouraged others to come west by offering them covered wagons.

ANSWER: BRIGHAM YOUNG (1801–1877)

Oklahoma

46th *State* ★ *November 16, 1907*

► Oklahoma comes from Choctaw words meaning "red people."

From 500 to 1300 A.D., Oklahoma Indians known as Mound Builders lived a sophisticated life until they mysteriously disappeared. The land was virtually free of people for hundreds of years until Europeans began to enter the region. The state's recorded history began in 1541 when Spanish explorer Francisco Vásquez de Coronado came through on his quest for the "Lost City of Gold." The 1803 Louisiana Purchase made the land part of the U.S.

The land was officially set aside as Indian Territory in 1834. Since the 1820s, the Five Civilized Tribes from the southeastern United States had been forced to move there. The relocation required people to walk thousands of miles over land routes such as the famous Cherokee Trail of Tears. The tribes suffered many hardships and losses along the way but soon established themselves in their new home. When the western portion of the territory was opened

▼ Clouds of dust roll over a ranch during the Oklahoma Dust Bowl of the 1930s.

◄ Today there are 39 different Indian tribes headquartered in Oklahoma.

to non-Indian settlers in 1889, thousands of people, including freed slaves, rushed the area to stake claims to land.

When oil was discovered, statehood was assured. Newcomers flocked to the region to seek their fortunes, and in 1907 Oklahoma joined the Union. Today oil, gas, and the services around energy still drive much of the state's industrial revenues. ✪

Did You Know?

At the time of statehood, African Americans outnumbered both Native Americans and people of European descent in Oklahoma. The state had more all-black towns than the rest of the U.S. combined.

Earth Alert! ►
In 2004 an Oklahoma man turned an old farm into a nesting ground for the least interior tern.

Mystery Person This ballet dancer was ► born in Fairfax, OK, in 1925. She was raised on the Osage Indian reservation and grew up to be America's most famous ballerina. She danced with the New York City Ballet for 18 years. In 1953 President Eisenhower named her "Woman of the Year."

ANSWER: MARIA TALLCHIEF (1925)

53

New Mexico

47th *State* ★ *January 6, 1912*

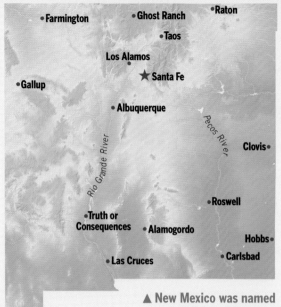

▲ New Mexico was named for the country of Mexico, of which it was once a part.

ndians have lived in New Mexico for at least 10,000 years. One ancient group, the Anasazi, raised crops in the desert and built large stone dwellings on the cliffs and in the canyons.

Spanish explorers saw New Mexico for the first time in the early 1500s and tried to colonize it. But the land was isolated at the edge of the Spanish empire, and the colony grew slowly. It became part of Mexico in 1821. When Mexico lost its northern lands in the Mexican-American War in 1848, it was transferred to the U.S.

Confederate troops took over much of the territory at the start of the Civil War. The Union army recaptured it in 1862, and the following decades were a time of conflict. American newcomers and local Navajo made peace in the late 1860s. But hostilities with some Apaches continued until their leader, Geronimo, surrendered in 1886. Disputes among cattle and sheep ranchers, homesteaders, and others erupted in violence in the 1870s and 1880s. Outlaws spread fear until federal lawmen established order.

New Mexico became a state in 1912. Since then, it has been a leader in nuclear and space research. Tourism is also important, as vacationers visit the state's spectacular deserts and mountains, and rich Indian and Spanish cultural sites. ✪

Did You Know?

Santa Fe is North America's longest continuously used seat of government, dating from about 1610.

▲ A multilevel pueblo, made of adobe, in Taos, NM

▶ The Albuquerque International Balloon Fiesta is a colorful event.

Earth Alert! ▶
Jaguars usually live in tropical regions, but some make their home in the American Southwest.

Mystery Person For much of her life, ▶ this artist lived and worked in the New Mexico desert. At her home in Ghost Ranch she created large-scale paintings of flowers and sun-bleached bones. There is a museum in Santa Fe dedicated to her work.

54

ANSWER: GEORGIA O'KEEFFE (1887–1986)

Arizona

48th *State* ★ *February 14, 1912*

Anasazi Indians built canals to water the Arizona desert more than 1,000 years before the first Spanish explorers arrived. Marcos De Niza passed through in 1539. Francisco Vásquez de Coronado followed in 1540 looking for cities of gold.

The Spanish set up Catholic missions in the 1600s and early 1700s. They founded their first settlement at Tubac in 1752.

Arizona was part of Mexico, which became independent from Spain in 1821. It remained a thinly populated region on Mexico's northern frontier until the U.S. gained control of the area in 1848 after winning the Mexican-American War.

The discovery of gold, silver, and copper in the late 1800s attracted more settlers. Railroad links across the region helped bring them in. Arizona became a state in 1912, but its growth was limited by its heat and dryness.

▶ Arizona comes from *arizonac*, an Indian word meaning "place of the little spring."

The U.S. government helped to bring water to the desert. Dams, including the huge Hoover Dam completed in 1935, created electricity and helped to water farms. Cotton became an important crop.

Arizona's population grew during World Wars I and II. By the 1960s, the widespread use of air conditioning made desert living more comfortable. As a result, many people moved to Arizona for its sunshine and warm climate. Today it is one of the nation's fastest-growing states. ✪

Completed in 1797, San Xavier del Bac Mission, near Tucson, still serves the public today.

Did You Know?

Indian reservations cover more than one-quarter of Arizona's land.

◀ Grand Canyon National Park in northern Arizona

Earth Alert! ▶
The Pima pineapple cactus grows in Arizona's Sonoran Desert. Its fruit is edible.

Mystery Person ▶
Born near Yuma, AZ, to immigrant parents, this labor leader is best known for organizing a long boycott against California grape growers. As executive director of United Farm Workers, he helped secure safer conditions, better pay, and union contracts for migrant workers.

ANSWER: CESAR CHAVEZ (1927-1993)

Alaska

Alaska's native people—Athabascans, Yupiks, and Aleuts—arrived from Asia at least 15,000 years ago. They had this vast land to themselves until 1784 when the Russians established a settlement on Kodiak Island, setting up fur trading posts, mining for coal, fishing, and hunting whales. But no more than 900 settlers ever lived in the territory at any one time. By the 1860s, Russia was eager to sell the land. The U.S. bought it in 1867 for $7,200,000—about two cents an acre.

The territory grew slowly until the discovery of large gold deposits in the late 1800s. Thousands of miners traveled to this remote region to strike it rich. Still, in 1900 Alaska was sparsely populated. It became the 49th state in 1959.

Alaska is still a wide-open frontier with only about one person per square mile. Jobs and revenue come mostly from timber, fishing, tourism, and oil. In 1967 the largest oil field in North America was found in the Arctic at Prudhoe Bay. Juneau is located in the world's northernmost rainforest. Just miles from the city, visitors can see glaciers, hike mountains, and relax at the beach. The challenge for Alaskans today is to use the state's valuable resources while protecting its unique wilderness. ★

◄ Alaska's name comes from the Aleut word *Alyeska*, which means "great land."

► Traditionally, native Alaskans carve totem poles from single tree trunks.

Did You Know?

In the northernmost part of Alaska, the sun never sets between May 10 and August 2.

► In 1867 Russia officially transferred Alaska to the U.S. in Sitka (seen here in the early 1900s).

Earth Alert! ►
The markings around its eyes make the spectacled eider look like it's wearing glasses.

Mystery Person ►
She was born in Boston but moved to Alaska when she was twenty years old. She is a four-time winner of the Iditarod, a 1,158-mile sled dog race across the Alaskan wilderness, from Anchorage to Nome. Today she raises huskies at her home in Eureka.

ANSWER: SUSAN BUTCHER (1954)

Hawaii

50th State ★ August 21, 1959

Lihue • Kapaa
Niihau   Kauai

• Haleiwa
Oahu
★ Honolulu

▼ The state's name may have come from *Hawaiki*, the name of a South Pacific island from which some of the first people came.

Molokai
Lanai **Lahaina**   Maui
Lanai   **Wailuku**
City
Kahoolawe

Hawaii
Hilo
• Kailua-Kona
Hawaii
Volcanoes
National
Park
Ka Lae

Polynesian people reached the Hawaiian Islands about 2,000 years ago. British explorer James Cook arrived in 1778—the first European to see Hawaii. Other explorers and traders soon followed. Eventually Hawaii became a water and supply stop for ships crossing the Pacific. American whaling ships began to dock here in the early 1800s. Missionaries came in 1820.

Large-scale farming on the islands' rich volcanic soil began in 1825 when Americans started the first sugar plantation. With a shortage of local labor, people were brought in from China, Japan, Portugal, and the Philippines to work the fields.

By the middle of the 19th century, the native Hawaiian population was dwindling. Newcomers carried diseases for which the islanders had no immunity. Many died. There were about

▲ Surfing is a popular sport in Hawaii.

Did You Know?
The Hawaiian Islands are actually the tops of volcanoes sticking out of the ocean.

300,000 native Hawaiians when Cook arrived. By 1853, only about 70,000 remained.

In the late 1800s, American farm and business owners were very powerful. They forced Queen Liliuokalani from power in 1893. The following year they declared Hawaii a republic. Hawaii became a U.S. territory in 1900. After decades of work by local leaders, Hawaii became a state in 1959.

Agriculture remains important in Hawaii. But spectacular beaches, volcanic mountains, and lush forests have made tourism key to the state's economy. ✪

▼ A Hawaiian pineapple plantation in the 1920s

Earth Alert! ▶
The Hawaiian gardenia is a small tree with shiny green leaves and fragrant white flowers.

Mystery Person The first in a long ▶ line of Hawaiian monarchs, this king became ruler of the Hawaiian Islands in 1810. He worked hard to preserve traditional customs and religious beliefs, even as traders began to settle on the islands. His family ruled for more than a century.

ANSWER: KING KAMEHAMEHA (1738-1819)

U.S. Territories &

Although they are not among the 50 states, there are several islands that are part of the United States. In some of these U.S. territories and commonwealths, the people are American citizens. In others they are not U.S. citizens but can enter the U.S. freely for work, education, or to live.

American officials have a say in how the territories and commonwealths are governed. Several of the territories control their local government while the U.S. handles foreign affairs. The commonwealths control most of their own internal affairs but still rely on the U.S. for protection and economic aid. Some of these islands have no permanent residents. They may be military facilities, research stations, or wildlife refuges. Take a look at these snapshots to learn more about the major U.S. territories and the two U.S. commonwealths. ★

NORTHERN Mariana Islands

The U.S. took the islands from Japan during World War II. In 1947 the U.N. gave the U.S. control over the Northern Marianas and two other Micronesian island groups, the Marshalls and the Carolines. The Northern Marianas chose to become a U.S. commonwealth in 1975. People of the Northern Marianas are American citizens but cannot vote in presidential elections.

AMERICAN Samoa

Status: Territory

Capital: Pago Pago

Population: 57,881; most people are Polynesian

Geography: Seven tiny islands in the South Pacific about 2,300 miles (3,700 km.) southwest of Hawaii; 77 sq. mi. (199 sq. km.)

Economy: Fishing, tuna canning

The U.S. established control over the Samoan Islands in the early 1900s. The people of American Samoa are not U.S. citizens, but they can enter and leave the U.S. without restrictions. American Samoa has a nonvoting delegate in the U.S. House of Representatives.

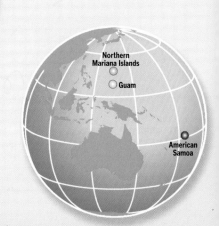

Northern Mariana Islands
Guam
American Samoa

Commonwealths

Guam

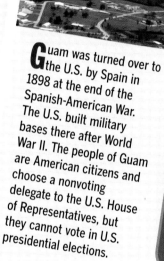

Status: Commonwealth

Capital: Saipan

Population: 80,362; mostly Asian and Pacific Islanders

Geography: A group of 16 western Pacific islands south of Japan and east of the Philippines; 184 sq. mi. (477 sq. km.)

Economy: tourism, government employment, textiles, farming, and fishing

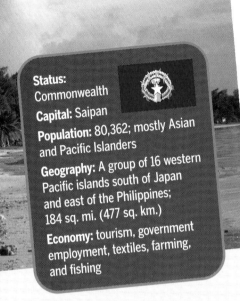

Guam was turned over to the U.S. by Spain in 1898 at the end of the Spanish-American War. The U.S. built military bases there after World War II. The people of Guam are American citizens and choose a nonvoting delegate to the U.S. House of Representatives, but they cannot vote in U.S. presidential elections.

Status: Territory

Capital: Hagatna

Population: 168,564; mostly native Chamorro (descendents of the original inhabitants from Southeast Asia) and Filipino

Geography: Island in the western Pacific; 212 sq. mi. (549 sq. km.)

Economy: tourism, U.S. military bases, fishing, and handicrafts

U.S. VIRGIN Islands

Status: Territory

Capital: Charlotte Amalie

Population: 108,708; mostly West Indian

Geography: A group of three main islands—St. Thomas, St. John, St. Croix—between the Atlantic Ocean and the Caribbean Sea; 134 sq. mi. (349 sq. km.)

Economy: Tourism, government employment, oil refining, aluminum ore (bauxite) refining, rum production

Denmark established settlements on the islands in the 1600s and early 1700s and controlled them until selling the islands to the United States in 1917. Many of the native people on the islands are of African descent. U.S. Virgin Islanders are American citizens and have one nonvoting delegate in the U.S. House of Representatives.

Puerto Rico   U.S. Virgin Islands

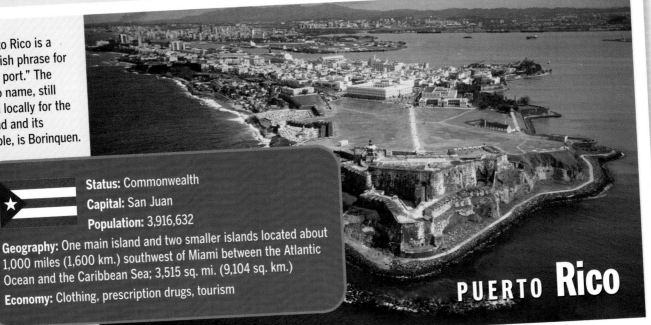

Puerto Rico is a Spanish phrase for "rich port." The Taino name, still used locally for the island and its people, is Borinquen.

Status: Commonwealth
Capital: San Juan
Population: 3,916,632
Geography: One main island and two smaller islands located about 1,000 miles (1,600 km.) southwest of Miami between the Atlantic Ocean and the Caribbean Sea; 3,515 sq. mi. (9,104 sq. km.)
Economy: Clothing, prescription drugs, tourism

PUERTO **Rico**

Puerto Rico's first inhabitants were the Taino Indians, who came from South America. Christopher Columbus reached the islands in 1493 and established Spain's claim. But European settlement didn't begin until 1508. Puerto Rico was ruled by Spain until 1898, when the Spanish gave it to the U.S. at the end of the Spanish-American War.

Puerto Rico became a U.S. territory in 1917, and a commonwealth on July 25, 1952. It is the largest and most important of the U.S. territories and commonwealths. The islands get protection and economic assistance from the U.S., but Puerto Rico's local government makes decision on local issues. Puerto Ricans are American citizens and serve in the U.S. armed forces. But they do not pay federal taxes and cannot vote in presidential elections. In the past few years Puerto Ricans have voted several times on whether or not to seek statehood. Islanders are split on the issue. Some want statehood, while others want complete independence from the U.S. Still, a majority of citizens have voted to maintain Puerto Rico's commonwealth status. ✪

Did You Know?

▼ President Theodore Roosevelt visited Puerto Rico on November 6, 1906, making him the first U.S. president to travel outside the country on official business.

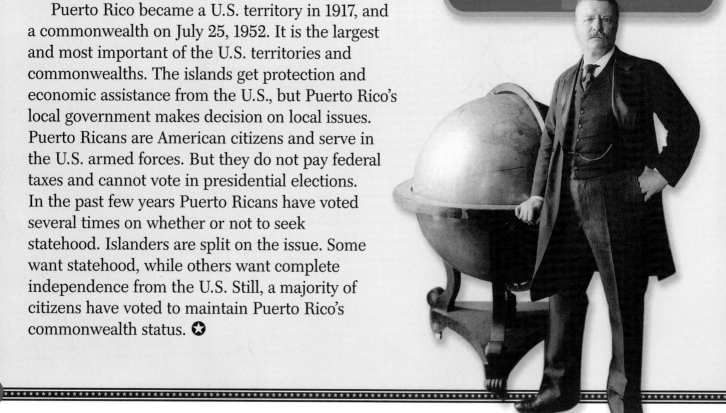

When the United States won its independence from Britain in 1789, Washington, DC, did not exist. But in 1800 the city became the nation's capital. George Washington picked the site for the city—an area of forest, farmland, and wetland where the Potomac and Anacostia Rivers meet. The land was part of Maryland, and the state turned it over to the federal government. French engineer Pierre Charles L'Enfant was hired to plan the city in 1791. He completed his work quickly, but many people found him to be difficult. Washington fired him the following year. L'Enfant left town and took the plans for the city with him. Luckily, African American surveyor and mathematician Benjamin Banneker was able to re-create the plans from memory. He and Andrew Ellicott finished the job. L'Enfant designed the city as a grid with the Capitol at its center; today the grid has 50 diagonal avenues, each named for a state.

Since the founding of their city, Washingtonians have had little say in how it's run. In 1961 the 23rd Amendment gave Washington residents the right to vote for president. In 1974 they got the right to elect their own local officials. But Washingtonians are still the only Americans without voting representatives in Congress.

▼ DC stands for District of Columbia, in honor of Christopher Columbus.

Washington is an unusual place. It has no industry or skyscrapers. Its main business is government. Yet its history and museums attract visitors from all over the world. ✪

OUR NATION'S CAPITAL
Washington, DC

The 50 States at a Glance

The first official U.S. flag was adopted by Congress on June 14, 1777. It looks different from the flag that flies today. It had just 13 stars, one for each state. Now our flag has 50 stars.

Over the years the American flag has changed many times. In 1794 two stars were added when Vermont and Kentucky joined the Union. It wasn't updated again until 1818. Seven stars were added, and Congress passed a bill saying that new stars would be added to the flag on the July 4th following the admission of a new state.

Every state has its own flag too. Stars, stripes, and the colors red, white, and blue are often used in the design. ★

ALABAMA #22

Postal Code: AL
Capital: Montgomery
Nickname: Heart of Dixie
Population: 4,530,182

Land Area: 50,750 sq. mi. (131,443 sq. km.)
State Symbols: *Game bird* wild turkey; *Rock* marble; *Nut* pecan

ALASKA #49

Postal Code: AK
Capital: Juneau
Nickname: Last Frontier
Population: 655,435

Land Area: 570,374 sq. mi. (1,477,267 sq. km.)
State Symbols: *Tree* Sitka spruce; *Flower* forget-me-not; *Sport* dog mushing

ARIZONA #48

Postal Code: AZ
Capital: Phoenix
Nickname: Grand Canyon State
Population: 5,743,834

Land Area: 113,642 sq. mi. (296,400 sq. km.)
State Symbols: *Fossil* petrified wood; *Gemstone* turquoise; *Fish* Arizona trout

ARKANSAS #25

Postal Code: AR
Capital: Little Rock
Nickname: Natural State
Population: 2,752,629

Land Area: 52,075 sq. mi. (134,874 sq. km.)
State Symbols: *Mammal* white-tailed deer; *Fish* largemouth bass; *Instrument* fiddle

CALIFORNIA #31

Postal Code: CA
Capital: Sacramento
Nickname: Golden State
Population: 35,893,799

Land Area: 155,973 sq. mi. (403,970 sq. km.)
State Symbols: *Tree* California redwood; *Bird* California valley quail

COLORADO #38

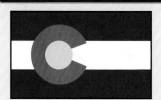

Postal Code: CO
Capital: Denver
Nickname: Centennial State
Population: 4,601,403

Land Area: 103,730 sq. mi. (269,618 sq. km.)
State Symbols: *Bird* lark bunting; *Animal* Rocky Mountain bighorn sheep

CONNECTICUT #5

Postal Code: CT

Capital: Hartford

Nickname: Constitution State

Population: 3,503,604

Land Area: 4,845 sq. mi. (12,550 sq. km.)

State Symbols: *Bird* American robin; *Flower* mountain laurel; *Shellfish* eastern oyster

DELAWARE #1

DECEMBER 7, 1787

Postal Code: DE

Capital: Dover

Nickname: First State

Population: 830,364

Land Area: 1,955 sq. mi. (5,153 sq. km.)

State Symbols: *Tree* American holly; *Insect* ladybug; *Beverage* milk

FLORIDA #27

Postal Code: FL

Capital: Tallahassee

Nickname: Sunshine State

Population: 17,397,161

Land Area: 54,153 sq. mi. (140,256 sq. km.)

State Symbols: *Salt water mammal* dolphin; *Reptile* alligator; *Gemstone* moonstone

GEORGIA #4

Postal Code: GA

Capital: Atlanta

Nickname: Peach State

Population: 8,829,383

Land Area: 57,919 sq. mi. (150,010 sq. km.)

State Symbols: *Tree* live oak; *Marine mammal* right whale; *Fossil* shark tooth

HAWAII #50

Postal Code: HI

Capital: Honolulu

Nickname: Aloha State

Population: 1,262,840

Land Area: 6,423 sq. mi. (16,637 sq. km.)

State Symbols: *Tree* kukui; *Bird* nene or Hawaiian goose; *Flower* yellow hibiscus

IDAHO #43

Postal Code: ID

Capital: Boise

Nickname: Gem State

Population: 1,393,262

Land Area: 82,751 sq. mi. (214,325 sq. km.)

State Symbols: *Tree* western white pine; *Bird* mountain bluebird; *Vegetable* potato

ILLINOIS #21

ILLINOIS

Postal Code: IL

Capital: Springfield

Nickname: Land of Lincoln

Population: 12,713,634

Land Area: 55,593 sq. mi. (143,987 sq. km.)

State Symbols: *Tree* white oak; *Fish* bluegill; *Snack* popcorn

INDIANA #19

Postal Code: IN

Capital: Indianapolis

Nickname: Hoosier State

Population: 6,237,569

Land Area: 35,870 sq. mi. (92,904 sq. km.)

State Symbols: *Tree* tulip tree; *Stone* limestone; *Flower* peony

IOWA #29

IOWA

Postal Code: IA

Capital: Des Moines

Nickname: Hawkeye State

Population: 2,954,451

Land Area: 55,875 sq. mi. (144,716 sq. km.)

State Symbols: *Tree* oak; *Bird* eastern goldfinch; *Flower* wild rose

KANSAS #34

KANSAS

Postal Code: KS

Capital: Topeka

Nickname: Sunflower State

Population: 2,735,502

Land Area: 81,823 sq. mi. (211,922 sq. km.)

State Symbols: *Bird* western meadowlark; *Animal* buffalo; *Flower* native sunflower

KENTUCKY #15

Postal Code: KY

Capital: Frankfort

Nickname: Bluegrass State

Population: 4,145,922

Land Area: 39,732 sq. mi. (102,907 sq. km.)

State Symbols: *Bird* Kentucky cardinal; *Horse* thoroughbred; *Gemstone* freshwater pearl

LOUISIANA #18

Postal Code: LA

Capital: Baton Rouge

Nickname: Pelican State

Population: 4,515,770

Land Area: 43,566 sq. mi. (112,836 sq. km.)

State Symbols: *Insect* honeybee; *Amphibian* green tree frog; *Flower* magnolia

MAINE #23

Postal Code: ME

Capital: Augusta

Nickname: Pine Tree State

Population: 1,317,253

Land Area: 30,865 sq. mi. (79,939 sq. km.)

State Symbols: *Herb* wintergreen; *Bird* chickadee; *Berry* wild blueberry

MARYLAND #7

Postal Code: MD

Capital: Annapolis

Nickname: Free State

Population: 5,558,058

Land Area: 9,775 sq. mi. (25,316 sq. km.)

State Symbols: *Fish* striped bass; *Flower* black-eyed Susan; *Team sport* lacrosse

MASSACHUSETTS #6

Postal Code: MA

Capital: Boston

Nickname: Bay State

Population: 6,416,505

Land Area: 7,838 sq. mi. (20,300 sq. km.)

State Symbols: *Game bird* wild turkey; *Fish* cod; *Dessert* Boston cream pie

MICHIGAN #26

Postal Code: MI

Capital: Lansing

Nickname: Wolverine State or Great Lake State

Population: 10,112,620

Land Area: 56,809 sq. mi. (147,135 sq. km.)

State Symbols: *Reptile* painted turtle; *Bird* robin; *Fish* brook trout

MINNESOTA #32

Postal Code: MN

Capital: St. Paul

Nickname: Gopher State

Population: 5,100,598

Land Area: 79,617 sq. mi. (206,207 sq. km.)

State Symbols: *Grain* wild rice; *Bird* common loon; *Muffin* blueberry

MISSISSIPPI #20

Postal Code: MS

Capital: Jackson

Nickname: Magnolia State

Population: 2,902,966

Land Area: 46,914 sq. mi. (121,506 sq. km.)

State Symbols: *Tree* magnolia; *Bird* mockingbird; *Flower* magnolia

MISSOURI #24

Postal Code: MO

Capital: Jefferson City

Nickname: Show-Me State

Population: 5,754,618

Land Area: 68,898 sq. mi. (178,446 sq. km.)

State Symbols: *Animal* Missouri mule; *Flower* white hawthorn; *Dinosaur* hadrosaur

MONTANA #41

Postal Code: MT

Capital: Helena

Nickname: Treasure State

Population: 926,865

Land Area: 145,556 sq. mi. (376,991 sq. km.)

State Symbols: *Tree* ponderosa pine; *Bird* western meadowlark; *Fish* cutthroat trout

NEBRASKA #37

Postal Code: NE

Capital: Lincoln

Nickname: Cornhusker State

Population: 1,747,214

Land Area: 76,878 sq. mi. (199,113 sq. km.)

State Symbols: *Tree* cottonwood; *Mammal* white-tailed deer; *Soft drink* Kool-Aid

NEVADA #36

Postal Code: NV

Capital: Carson City

Nickname: Silver State

Population: 2,334,771

Land Area: 109,806 sq. mi. (284,397 sq. km.)

State Symbols: *Bird* mountain bluebird; *Animal* desert bighorn sheep; *Metal* silver

NEW HAMPSHIRE #9

Postal Code: NH

Capital: Concord

Nickname: Golden State

Population: 1,299,500

Land Area: 8,969 sq. mi. (23,231 sq. km.)

State Symbols: *Tree* white birch; *Bird* purple finch; *Flower* purple lilac

NEW JERSEY #3

Postal Code: NJ

Capital: Trenton

Nickname: Garden State

Population: 8,698,879

Land Area: 7,419 sq.mi. (19,215 sq. km.)

State Symbols: *Tree* red oak; *Mammal* horse; *Flower* violet

NEW MEXICO #47

Postal Code: NM

Capital: Santa Fe

Nickname: Land of Enchantment

Population: 1,903,289

Land Area: 121,365 sq. mi. (314,334 sq. km.)

State Symbols: *Tree* piñon pine; *Bird* roadrunner; *Flower* yucca

NEW YORK #11

Postal Code: NY

Capital: Albany

Nickname: Empire State

Population: 19,227,088

Land Area: 47,224 sq. mi. (122,310 sq. km.)

State Symbols: *Mammal* beaver; *Shell* bay scallop; *Flower* rose

NORTH CAROLINA #12

Postal Code: NC

Capital: Raleigh

Nickname: Tar Heel State

Population: 8,541,221

Land Area: 48,718 sq. mi. (126,180 sq. km.)

State Symbols: *Tree* pine; *Fish* channel bass; *Vegetable* sweet potato

NORTH DAKOTA #39

Postal Code: ND

Capital: Bismarck

Nickname: Flickertail State

Population: 634,366

Land Area: 70,704 sq. mi. (183,123 sq. km.)

State Symbols: *Tree* American elm; *Bird* western meadowlark; *Flower* wild prairie rose

OHIO #17

Postal Code: OH

Capital: Columbus

Nickname: Buckeye State

Population: 11,459,011

Land Area: 40,953 sq. mi. (106,067 sq. km.)

State Symbols: *Bird* cardinal; *Beverage* tomato juice; *Flower* scarlet carnation

OKLAHOMA #46

Postal Code: OK

Capital: Oklahoma City

Nickname: Sooner State

Population: 3,511,532

Land Area: 68,679 sq. mi. (177,880 sq. km.)

State Symbols: *Tree* redbud; *Animal* bison; *Wildflower* Indian blanket

OREGON #33

Postal Code: OR

Capital: Salem

Nickname: Beaver State

Population: 3,594,586

Land Area: 96,003 sq. mi. (248,647 sq. km.)

State Symbols: *Tree* Douglas fir; *Fish* chinook salmon; *Flower* Oregon grape

PENNSYLVANIA #2

Postal Code: PA

Capital: Harrisburg

Nickname: Keystone State

Population: 12,406,292

Land Area: 44,820 sq. mi. (116,083 sq. km.)

State Symbols: *Tree* hemlock; *Bird* ruffled grouse; *Dog* Great Dane

RHODE ISLAND #13

Postal Code: RI

Capital: Providence

Nickname: Ocean State

Population: 1,080,632

Land Area: 1,045 sq. mi. (2,706 sq. km.)

State Symbols: *Tree* red maple; *Bird* Rhode Island red hen; *Flower* violet

SOUTH CAROLINA #8

Postal Code: SC

Capital: Columbia

Nickname: Palmetto State

Population: 4,198,086

Land Area: 30,111 sq. mi. (77,988 sq. km.)

State Symbols: *Reptile* loggerhead turtle; *Bird* Carolina wren; *Flower* yellow jessamine

SOUTH DAKOTA #40

Postal Code: SD

Capital: Pierre

Nickname: Mount Rushmore State

Population: 770,883

Land Area: 75,898 sq. mi. (196,575 sq. km.)

State Symbols: *Tree* Black Hills spruce; *Mineral* rose quartz; *Fossil* triceratops

TENNESSEE #16

Postal Code: TN

Capital: Nashville

Nickname: Volunteer State

Population: 5,900,962

Land Area: 41,220 sq. mi. (106,759 sq. km.)

State Symbols: *Bird* mockingbird; *Gemstone* Tennessee River pearl

TEXAS #28

Postal Code: TX

Capital: Austin

Nickname: Lone Star State

Population: 22,490,022

Land Area: 261,914 sq. mi. (678,358 sq. km.)

State Symbols: *Tree* pecan; *Reptile* horned lizard; *Large mammal* longhorn cattle

UTAH #45

Postal Code: UT

Capital: Salt Lake City

Nickname: Beehive State

Population: 2,389,039

Land Area: 82,168 sq. mi. (212,816 sq. km.)

State Symbols: *Tree* blue spruce; *Bird* California seagull; *Animal* mountain elk

VERMONT #14

Postal Code: VT

Capital: Montpelier

Nickname: Green Mountain State

Population: 621,394

Land Area: 9,249 sq. mi. (23,956 sq. km.)

State Symbols: *Tree* sugar maple; *Animal* Morgan horse; *Flower* red clover

VIRGINIA #10

Postal Code: VA

Capital: Richmond

Nickname: Old Dominion

Population: 7,459,827

Land Area: 39,598 sq. mi. (102,558 sq. km.)

State Symbols: *Dog* American fox hound; *Bird* cardinal; *Insect* tiger swallowtail butterfly

WASHINGTON #42

Postal Code: WA

Capital: Olympia

Nickname: Evergreen State

Population: 6,203,788

Land Area: 66,582 sq. mi. (17,447 sq. km.)

State Symbols: *Tree* western hemlock; *Fossil* Columbian mammoth

WEST VIRGINIA #35

Postal Code: WV

Capital: Charleston

Nickname: Mountain State

Population: 1,815,354

Land Area: 24,087 sq. mi. (62,384 sq. km.)

State Symbols: *Tree* sugar maple; *Soil* Monongahela silt loam; *Fruit* golden delicious apple

WISCONSIN #30

Postal Code: WI

Capital: Madison

Nickname: Badger State

Population: 5,509,026

Land Area: 54,314 sq. mi. (140,673 sq. km.)

State Symbols: *Stone* red granite; *Peace symbol* mourning dove; *Dance* polka

WYOMING #44

Postal Code: WY

Capital: Cheyenne

Nickname: Equality State

Population: 506,529

Land Area: 97,105 sq. mi. (251,501 sq. km.)

State Symbols: *Tree* cottonwood; *Bird* meadowlark; *Gemstone* jade

A History Mystery

id Betsy Ross make America's first flag? Legend has it that George Washington designed the flag, and that he secretly hired the Philadelphia seamstress after she showed him how to make a five-pointed star with one snip of the scissors. Betsy finished the flag in June 1776. It was unveiled the next month. There is no written proof that Betsy sewed the flag. But she was known to have made flags for ships during the American Revolution. In 1870 Betsy's grandson, William Canby, revealed her role in history. True or false, it's been a popular story ever since. ★

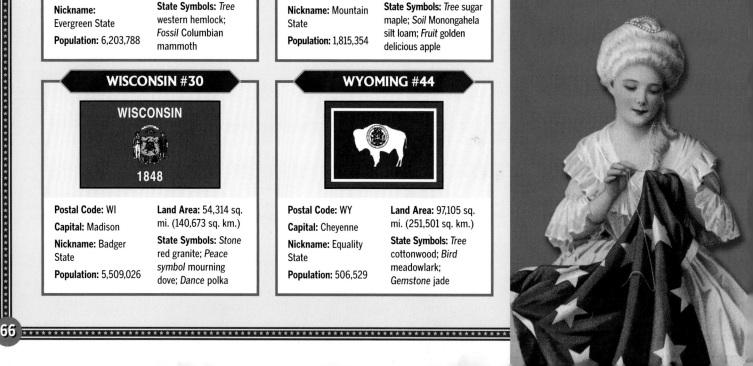

Index

State Mottoes

"Ua mau ke ea o ka aina I ka pono (The life of the land is perpetuated in righteousness)"
— HAWAII

"Equality before the law"
— NEBRASKA

"Alis volat propiis (She flies with her own wings)" — OREGON

"Equal rights"
— WYOMING

"Fatti maschii, parole femine (Manly deeds, womanly words)"
— MARYLAND

"Wisdom, justice, and moderation" — GEORGIA

"Our liberties we prize and our rights we will maintain"
— IOWA